Joseph!
I trust this book will be a blessing and an inspiration to you. Thanks for your support.

Love

[signature]

Originally published in 2019 by Amazon Publishing

Amazon Publishing
Seattle, WA

ISBN-13: 978-1-7186-8411-9
ISBN-10: 1-7186-8411-8

Printed and bound in the United States by CreateSpace, An Amazon.com Company

CONTENTS

Foreword

I count it a great honor to write these words as a foreword to this book by Abbie Thornton.

What I particularly like about this book is that it is a series of personal experiences over Abbie's life that has molded her thinking and transformed her thoughts to bring her to where she is today. We hold our destiny in our own hands, we should just be still and know that we are part of the universal thought, which is God.

I can only hope and pray that many believers will find this book coming into their hands and drawing from it the spiritual truth about your thoughts. Thank you for sharing your life's journey with us.

Tammy L. White, MBA, Information Technology Consultant of a multinational software corporation, and a Friend over 20 years.

Daily Confessions

I was working at Capital One in Richmond, VA in 2002 on a contract assignment. I spend most of my time at the Homewood Suites hotel. I attended this Church on a regular basis when I was there over the weekend. One Sunday they provided this daily confession and I have been confessing it since 2002.

Your Word says to put You in remembrance...... Isaiah 43:26
Jesus said that you have what you say..... Mark 11:23

This is the day that the Lord has made, I will rejoice and be glad in it. It is going to be a good day. I am a Covenant child. I hear the voice of the Good Shepherd and the voice of a stranger I will not follow. You oh God love me and have a wonderful plan for my life. Because I fear You, You will teach me to choose the best and I will live within my circle of blessing. I will be all You want me to be and have all You want me to have! **(Psalm 118:24, John 10:4, John 3:16, Psalm 25:12-13, Isaiah 29:11)**

Everything that I put my hand to will prosper. You give me the power to get wealth, that You may establish Your covenant with me. I am blessed coming in and blessed going out. You will go before me and make the mountains low and the valleys high and the crooked places straight. Favor compasses me about as a shield. I am the head and not the tail, above only and not beneath. You will fight with those who fight with me and I am more than a conqueror. No weapon formed against me will prosper, and who ever gathers together against me, it will not be by You, and they will fall for my sake. **(Psalm 1:3, Deuteronomy 28:13, Romans 8:37, Isaiah 54:17, Isaiah 54:15)**

I have wisdom and I have the peace of God that passes all understanding. I have the mind of Christ. I can do all things through Christ who strengthens me. **(James 1:5, Philippians 4:7, I Corinthian, Philippians 4:13)**

Angels of God encamp round about me and protect me. Goodness and mercy follow me all the days of my life and You give me favor!! You will guard and keep that which I have committed to You and protect that which concerns me. I have committed my children, my mother, sisters and brothers, aunts and uncles and all of their families, my friends, my enemies, my co-workers and those that spitefully use me to You; and I believe that You will protect and perfect them. The seed of the just is blessed!! **(Psalm 34:7, Psalm 23:6, II Timothy, Psalm 138:8, Isaiah 44:3)**

I do not fear because You have given me a spirit of love, power and a sound mind. My steps are ordered by the Lord and they are safe upright and happy steps that go in the right direction. **(II Timothy 1:7, Psalm 37:23, Hebrew 12:13)**

I prosper in every way and I am in good health even as my soul prosper. I am the righteousness of God in Christ Jesus and I flourish like a beautiful tree in the courts of my God and I will bring forth fruit in my old age. **(3 John 2, II Corinthians 5:21, Psalm 92:12-15)**

Jesus has come that I may have life, and that I may have it more abundantly and I receive it!! You will hasten Your Word to perform it and it will not return to You void. You cannot lie, and all of Your promises are Yea and Amen!!! **(John 10:10, Jeremiah 1:12, Isaiah 55:11, Hebrew 6:18, II Corinthians)**

Significance of 7

There is a seed that is planted within you that eventually germinates and blooms into that which you were sent to this earth to be and to accomplish. I was born to a single mother with nine children. I was number seven out of the nine. In the Bible, the number 7 represents completeness and perfection (both physically and spiritually). It derives much of its meaning from being tied directly to God's creation of everything.   God created the heavens and earth in 7 days. In the book of Revelation, there are 7 churches (Ephesus, Smyrna, Pergamos, Thyatira, Sardis, Philadelphia, and Laodiceans); 7 seals; 7 angels; and 7 trumpet plagues. The number 7 is the seeker, the thinker and the searcher of Truth. The number 7 knows that nothing is exactly as it seems, and that reality is often hidden behind illusions.

Below is a chart of my Mother and her children. I have listed the month and year of their birth, along with their initials.

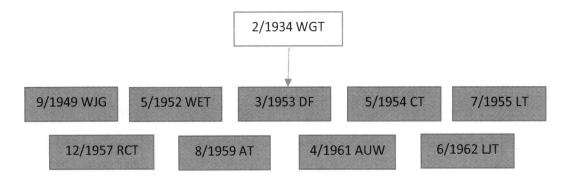

Junk Food vs Natural Food

My Mother worked for the Dismukes' (Sylvia and Wilbur). She would clean their house and take care of their two young girls, Donna and Dana. My Mother was paid $5 a week. Mr. Dismuke worked for Tom's Snacks Company. He delivered chips and snack foods to stores. As Mr. Dismuke traded out old and expired food in the stores, he would give the old and expired food snacks to my Mother. She would bring it home to us to eat, and we thought we had died and gone to heaven. In hindsight, all that junk food has contributed to individuals dying with various diseases and they have subsequently gone to heaven.

When we were growing up, we could not afford to by junk food such as chips, crackers, candy etc. Everything we ate was either grown in the fields, on trees or raised (e.g. corn, peas, okra, chicken, pigs, fruit, etc.).

Around our house and within our community, we had an abundance of apples, pears, peaches, pecans, muscadines, plums, strawberries, blackberries, figs etc., and they were only a skip and a hop away. We did not hunger for anything.

Primary School "Daze"

I attended Aberfoil School's Head Start Program and I also attended the first and second grade there. Our school had three (3) rooms that housed the students in the community. There were 3 grades in each room, and one instructor. One room had grades 1-3, the second room had grades 4-6, the third room had grade 7-9. Students that were in grades 10-12 attended the Technical High School in Perote, Alabama. There was another room that was used for gathering of the entire student body and other activities (e.g., assembly programs, lunchroom, Sock-Hop dances). Our parents would attend these dances with us, and it cost about a dime in the 1960s.

Each room had a coal/wood burning stove to warm the room in the winter, and a wooden floor. During the spring and summer months, the window would be raised to let fresh air into the building. During this time, we did not have any air conditioner, maybe a fan in the window. We walked to school each day, which was approximately ½ mile from where I lived.

The government provided milk, juice and some snacks through the Head Start Program and the free breakfast program. I remember breakfast being milk and cereal. It seems as if we had to bring our lunch. I recall having Peanut Butter and Crackers sandwiches.

My teacher was Mrs. McGowan and she taught grades 1-3. When I was in the first grade, Mrs. McGowan had a conversation with my Mother about potentially skipping me a grade due to me being much further ahead of my class. I was a fast learner. However, my Mother did not agree to this, and I don't know why. So, I remained with my first-grade class. Nevertheless, when I was in the second-grade class, Mrs. McGowan would allow me to teach the first-grade, while she was teaching the third-grade class. Can you imagine that?

Visit by the Governor

After being promoted to third grade, the schools were integrated, and we were bused to South Highland Elementary School in 1967. While I was in the third grade, we had a visit from the Governor of the state of Alabama, who at the time was Lurleen B.Wallace. Lurleen B. Wallace was the wife of George Wallace, who had been the Governor for the preceding four years. After Lurleen B. Wallace's visit to South Highland Elementary School, there was an article that was written by the Union Springs Herald newspaper about her visit, and I was mentioned in that article. I was 8 years old at the time. I am still trying to locate that article to determine exactly what was written. I am sure it is somewhere in my Mother's house. I vaguely remember my Mother putting the article in the Bible.

South Highland Middle School

South Highland Elementary School name was later changed to South Highland Middle School, and it housed grades 4-6. I was in this play at this school one day, and we had to learn the "State's Song". I would later dream of visiting these state one day. Here is the song:
1. Why did Alabama boys? Oh, I don't know Alaska.
2. What did Mississippi boys? She sipped a Minnesota.
3. What did Idaho boys? She hoed a Maryland.
4. What did Delaware boys? She wore a brand New Jersey.
5. What did Tennessee boys? They saw what Arkansas.
6. Why did California boys? They phoned to say Hawaii.
7. What did Iowa (Ioweigh) boys? She weighed a Washington.
8. How did Florida (Floradie) boys? She died in Missouri.
9. Where has Oregon boys? She's gone to Oklahoma. She went to pay her Texas (taxes)
10. How did Wisconsin boys? She stole a Nebraska.

As of the writing of this book, I have visited all these states except Alaska, Idaho, and Oregon. Of course, I lived in Alabama at the time. While in college and after starting to work, I visited a friend in Jackson, Mississippi while working near Mississippi for Sara Lee Hosiery. I visited the Mall of America in Minneapolis, Minnesota while attending a conference. I lived in Silver Springs, Maryland while doing Co-op with the Department of Health and Human Services my senior year in College. I attended a continuing education conference and we took a trip down the Delaware River. While working in Philadelphia, New Jersey was right across the way. Our family had Christmas one years in Nashville, Tennessee and well as me working there for a company that had a subsidiary in Tennessee. One of my friends was from Arkansas and I attended her Mother's funeral. I worked in California while working at Duke Power Company on a major contract we had with a company that was based in San Francisco California. I have also had a few vacations and attended conferences in California. I spend my 50th birthday in Honolulu Hawaii. I worked on a contract job in Des Moines Iowa in 2017. While working at VF Corporation, we had offices in the state of Washington where I worked on a project in Seattle. I have vacationed in Florida several times. I worked with the IIA on a project in St. Louis Missouri at Emerson Electric. I traveled through Oklahoma on the way to Omaha, Nebraska to help find my nephew an apartment to live in before starting his new job with the government. I have worked in Houston Texas at one of Ashland Oil's subsidiaries while working at Ashland Oil Company. I worked in Appleton Wisconsin at Jan Sports which was one of VF Corporation's subsidiaries.

One of the main events of the school year was May Day celebration. This was a day that the parents took off from work and visited the school. We got new outfits to wear to school that day. The outfit was usually a white t-shirt and a pair of shorts. There were lots of games, food and activities. One of the main activities was the "Wrapping of the May Pole". There were these long strings of material of different colors attached to the top of the pole. We would practice for days to ensure we would wrap the May Pole properly. Some of the teachers that left a memorable impression on me were Ms. Chilton, Ms. Meadow, Ms. Williams and Mr. Calloway, our physical education teacher. The Principal was name Mr. Price and his secretary was Ms. Bush. We were disciplined using a "leather strap" from grades 1 to 9. I have been at the end of that "strap" several times.

4-H Club

When attending South Highland Middle School, (grades 4-6), I was a member of the 4-H Club. 4-H is a global network of youth organizations whose mission is engaging youth to reach their fullest potential while advancing the field of youth development. Its name is a reference to the occurrences of the initial letter "H" four times in the organization's original motto; head, heart, hands and health, which was later incorporated in the fuller pledge officially adopted in 1927.

Pledge
I pledge my 'head' to clear thinking,
My 'heart' to greater loyalty,
My 'hands; to larger service,
and my 'health' to better living,
for my club, my community, my country and my world.

In the US, the organization is administered by the National Institute of Food and Agricultural of the U.S. Department of Agricultural (USDA).

The goal of the 4-H is to develop citizenship, leadership, responsibility and life skills of youth through experimental learning programs and a positive youth development approach.

The 4-H motto is "To Make the Best Better" while its slogan is "Learn by Doing".

Ms. Rosa was over the 4-H program in our community and/or district. I was selected to go with Mrs. Rosa to one of the district meetings, which was in Auburn Alabama. I was the only black student at the meeting and was in grade 5 or 6.

After attending the district meeting, I remember going to the local radio station with Mrs. Rosa to read an article related to the 4-H on the radio station in Union Springs, Alabama.

Motivation: *Look at the wonder of that which is before you.*

Decade 2: Age 11-20 *(1970 – 1979)*
Chapter 2 - Forgetting Those Things Behind You

Philippians 3:13-14

> *13. Brethren, I count not myself to have apprehended; but this one thing I do, forgetting those things which are behind, and reaching forth unto those things, which are before.*
> *14. I press toward the mark for the prize of the high calling of God in Christ Jesus.*

I believe in always looking forward. When a situation does not go as I had hoped or planned, I would always say that the Lord has something better for me.

When a relationship ends, I throw away any pictures or items that may remind me of that relationship. I try not to keep any picture of past relationships. Nevertheless, I may still have a cordial relationship or friendship with that person, but I am currently not the person that I was when I was with them in that relationship. I have moved on mentally and I have no desire to hold on to any memories whether good or bad. I believe that part of my life is non-existence now. The lesson has been learned, or the purpose for them being in my life has been fulfilled. I believe that the door should be closed on the old so that a new door can opened.

I remember when I was in the 7th Grade, this guy that I considered as my boyfriend had given me my birth stone ring. One day, he called and told me that he was "quitting me", which meant we were no longer girlfriend and boyfriend. I was so hurt, and I flushed the ring he had given me down the commode. However, the next day he wanted to get back together. It was too late.

Any job that you may lose, or relationship that may end, always know that the Lord has something better for you somewhere else. Sometimes doors must be closed so that you can see the blessing ahead of you. I currently work on a contract basis, and when my contract job has ended, I look forward to a new contract with another company. There are times when I may return to the same company, but it is a new contract.

Junior High

Mr. Ashley, my 9th grade Algebra teacher used to always tell me that I was going to be very successful. He told three of my close friends that Thornton is going to be driving by them in her car while they are on the side of the road, in a ditch. I used to envision myself driving along the road in my new car, but not passing by them in the ditch. That vision stuck in my mind when I was in the 9th grade. Of course, my friends have led different lives from me. Two of them went on to obtain college degrees. All three friends have been or is currently married. As of the publishing of this book, I am currently single.

The following writing was sent to me for Mother's Day one year by a friend of mine. I have kept this on my refrigerator for several years and have read it often. I think that this is so very appropriate as we go through this life.

God's Plan for our Lives

God has a plan for me. It is hidden within me, just as the oak is hidden within the acorn, or the rose within the bud. I believe that anything which comes into my life is necessary for my growth. As I give myself more fully to this God-given plan, it expresses itself more perfectly through me. I can tell when I am in tune with it, for then my mind and heart are filled with a deep inner peace. This peace fills me with a sense of security, with joy, and a desire to do those things that are a part of the Plan; or I am filled with a new patience, a new stillness, that make it possible for other to unfold the Plan to me.

This Plan is a perfect part of a larger Plan, it is designed for the good of all and not for me alone. It is a many-sided Plan and reaches out through all the people I meet and all the events of my life, therefore I accept the events and the people who come into my life as instruments for the unfolding of God's Plan for me.

God has chosen those he wants me to know, to love and to serve, and we are continually being drawn to one another. I pray that I may become a better instrument to love and to serve and that I may become more worthy to receive the love and service of others, so that together we may more perfectly express God's Plan in our lives.

I ask the Father within for only those things which are mine. I know that my good will come to me at the right time and in the right way. This inner knowing frees my mind and heart from all fear, jealousy, anger and resentment. It gives me courage and faith to do those things which I feel are mine to do. When I am in tune with God's Plan, I am free from greed, passion, impure thoughts and deeds. I no longer look with envy at what other are receiving nor do I compare myself with them. Therefore, I do not cut myself off from God, the giver of all good things.

God's gifts to me are many, many times greater than I am now receiving. I pray that I may increase my capacity to receive as well as my ability to give, for I can give only as I receive and receive only as I give. The gifts of God always bring peace, harmony and joy. So, anything that fill me with peace and harmony and does not hurt another is God-given and belongs to me. I believe that any work I feel called upon to do is mine to do. When I am in tune with that which is truly mine, all things work together for the good of all.

I believe that when I cannot do those things I desire to do, it is because God has closed the door only to open another, a better, larger door. If I do not see the door just ahead, it is because I have not seen, heard or obeyed God's guidance. It is then that God uses the trouble or seeming failure which may result to help me face myself and find the inspiration and power to see the right door.

The real purpose of my life is to find God within my own mind and heart and to help my fellow men. His Love, Light and Life will be expressed more perfectly through me, as I keep in touch with the Father. I pray that I may always be grateful for the countless expressions of His Love, Harmony and Beauty and for His unfailing guidance. I thank my heavenly Father for each experience which helps me to surrender my will to His Will and brings me closer to Him. For only as I lose myself in the consciousness of His great presence can His Plan for my life be fulfilled.

Author: Anonymous

Motivation: *Visualize the results you want.*

Summer Jobs

During the Summer of 1972, I got my first job working on the summer program for less fortunate and low-income families. My older sister and I would have to get up early in the morning, so that our Mother could drop us off at the Recreation Center on her way to work. We were usually at the Center at least an hour before it opened. We would just sit outside on the benches until the Director (Cousin Smokey) would open the Center. Sometimes, we would go to sleep while waiting for the Center to open.

The Recreation Center had this huge pool. I wanted to get in it, but could not swim, and probably didn't have a swimsuit. My job was to mainly clean-up around the recreational center and keep things in order.

The next summer of 1973, I worked at the Tax Accessor's Office in the County Courthouse with Mrs. Aileen Blow. This consisted mainly of completing information in the "Deed of Records" book.

I worked at the Home Extension Services with Kathy Hill the summer of 1977 before going to college at Alabama State University. Kathy lived down the road below my Mother's house, and she had to pass by our house on her way to work. So, I would catch a ride with her to work every day. My role was to file correspondence, send out letters and accept payment on loans.

Delivery

On November 12, 1974, at the age of 15, I gave birth to my first daughter. I played softball while I was 6-7 months pregnant. This probably contributed to a pain free delivery. Of course, there was no such thing as an "epidural" when I gave birth, it was a natural delivery.

During this time, the mentality was that if you become pregnant that meant you had to drop out of school because it did not look good with a pregnant person being in school, as well as this was tarnishing to the family's image. So, I continued to go to school without my Mother's blessing. I could not ride the bus because my Mother had not left for work before the bus arrived; so, I had to wait until my Mother went to work to catch a ride to school. Sometimes I would just start to walk to school and crying along the way, and someone would stop to pick me up if they were going in that direction. The school was at least 5 miles from where we lived. When my Mother would get home from work, and if she found out that I had gone to school that day, I would get disciplined. Of course, I continued to go to school every day. After a while, she stopped discipling me.

The Church also looked down on a person that was pregnant out of wedlock. I continued to go to church every Sunday hoping that someone would verbally try to judge me. My intent was to call out their sins and judge them in return. I knew that we were all sinners and my sin was no greater than theirs. Nevertheless, no one ever judged me openly or in my presence.

Welfare

I applied for welfare when I was pregnant and started receiving $59 a month. Every so often, I had to go back to the welfare office to requalify for the $59 a month. The last time that I went to requalify, I got so pissed off and said to myself that, "I am going to make more money than any of you in this office."

A friend of mine sent me the following poem one Mother's Day and I am including it here because I think it is most appropriate.

A Mother's Love

A halo that reflects a life of wisdom, kindness, and caring.
Eyes that sparkle with pride and show how much she believes in you.
Shoulders that have been slept and wept on and carried a world or two.
Arms that never run out of hugs.
Hands that know just when to let go.
A mind filled with amazing things, from fairy tales to family tails and long-ago stories of you.
A smile that can jump right into your heart and warm you faster than hot chocolate.
A heart of gold that holds more love than you can image.
That's what a mother is and so much more!!
Celebrate each and every day because Mother's make the world go around.

High School

After I gave birth to my first daughter, I was probably out of school for at least 6 weeks. During this time, I missed a lot of my homework assignments. However, upon returning to school, I made up my homework, took the related tests and was able to get a passing grade in all of my courses. Even with me missing 6 weeks of school, in May 1977, I still graduated as Salutatorian from my class, with only one point different from the person that was the Valedictorian.

When I was a senior in High School, I became a majorette in the Marching Band. We had an opportunity to travel to different schools to perform as well as participate in several activities, this included participating in the Madigras Parade in New Orleans. We toured the Super Dome which at that time was considered massive in my mind. We went to Six Flags Over Georgia in Atlanta, and we performed in Alabama State University's Turkey Day Classic Parade in Montgomery, Alabama.

Decisions, Decisions, Decisions

I took the ACT test which was a prerequisite to going to college. Of course, at the time my Mother was not able to pay for us to go to college. My older sisters had gone to college a year earlier. Due to our family being under the poverty level, we qualified for a Basic Education Opportunity Grant (BEOG) from the government. This grant provided full tuition, room and board and work study. I applied for attendance at various colleges in Alabama. I was accepted at Alabama State University, and in August of 1977, I started college at Alabama State University and decided to major in Accounting. I remember staying in Bibb Graves Hall, and one of my room mates' name was Cathy and the other one was Donna. Cathy was from Georgia and Donna pledge AKA. I wanted to pledge one of the sororities, but I could not comprehend participating in something that I considered to be foolish acts, (e.g., someone hitting on me and me not hitting them back; then later on we are the best of sisters). At the same time, I did not have the money that was required to pledge, and I knew my Mother did not have it either and if she did, she would not put it towards such an activity.

Income during Decade 2

Year	Source	Amount
1972	Summer Employment ($1.60 per Hour)	$388.80
1973	Summer Employment ($2.00 per Hour)	$504.00
1975	Aid to Dependent Children - Welfare ($59 per month)	$552.00
1976	Aid to Dependent Children - Welfare ($59 per month)	$552.00
1977	Aid to Dependent Children - Welfare ($59 per month); Summer Employment	$1,370.00
1978	Summer Employment	$636.00
1979	NA	$ 0.00
	Total	**$4,002.80**

Motivation: *Decide what you want. Tell someone your vision and dreams.*

Decade 3: Age 21-30 *(1980 – 1989)*
Chapter 4 – Straight "Otta" ASU

During the Fall of 1977, I started college at Alabama State University where I majored in Accounting.   We were poor by government standards and I went to college on a Basic Education Opportunity Grant (BEOG) which covered my tuition and room and board.

Dr. Percy J. Vaughn was the Dean of the College of Business Administration (COBA) and he was my idol and mentor. All the students in the College of Business were literally afraid of Dr. Vaughn. If we saw him coming down the hall, we would "straighten up and fly fight".

I took a Marketing class from Dr. Vaughn and we had to develop a product. I created a "Disaster Recovery Kit". As I look back on this class, I wonder if I should have marketed that kit back in 1979 or 1980. We left those products for display in the College of Business.

Work Study

I worked in ASU business office performing miscellaneous bookkeeping or accounting duties. There were a few times that I shadowed the cashiers at the Cashiers' window. When I was a Senior in College, I worked almost 40 hours a week in the ASU Business Office. Mr. Lewis was my supervisor and he had high hopes of me becoming a full-time employee after I graduated. Of course, that was not the direction I wanted to go in after graduation. One thing that I did not like about that office, was that it was so cold in the summertime, and I felt that the temperature was set to mainly appeased Mr. Lewis.   Every day, I would leave with a headache and was so uncomfortable while working there. My sinuses were inflamed, and I felt miserable. Greg, Mary, Winston and Dorothy were some of my co-workers that I enjoyed working with.

Transportation Woes

On February 25, 1980, I gave birth to my second daughter. After giving birth to my second daughter, I started commuting to college each day. I lived an hour drive away from Alabama State University. Some days I caught the Grey Hound Bus to Montgomery. Other days, I would "hitch" a ride with some other student that lived in Union Springs, Alabama and were commuting to Montgomery everyday also. One day my sister and I "caught" a ride with William during the winter months. William did not have any heat in his car, and my feet felt like they were outside of the car, and they were just freezing to death. William did not have class every day, so I had to find someone else to catch a ride with, when William was not commuting to school.

I found that another person by the name of Fitzgerald was driving to ASU each day, so I started riding with Fitzgerald. Of course, I paid William and Fitzgerald to ride with them. I lived 5 miles out of William and Fitzgerald's way. One morning, I was waiting at home for Fitzgerald to pick me up and he never showed up. Somehow, I was able to get to the Grey Hound Bus stop before the bus left Union Springs going to Montgomery. I arrived on the Campus in enough time to get to my class on time. As I am walking down the hall, the first person I saw was Fitzgerald. I always speak to everyone that crosses my path. After I spoke to Fitzgerald, it dawned on me that Fitzgerald had not come to pick me up that morning. That was probably the last time I saw Fitzgerald or had any type of interaction with Fitzgerald. Then in March 2018, thirty-eight years later, I saw Fitzgerald at the funeral of a friend of mine. I made no effort to speak to him as I was relaying the above story to a friend of mine that was sitting beside me at the funeral.

Subsequently, after experiencing the challenges of trying to get to school each day, I decided to buy me a car. I didn't know how I was going to pay for it, but the Lord made a way. In 1980, I bought my first car, Mazda GLC. I did not know how to drive a manual shift. The first day me and my sister went to school in the new car, we got off on an exit and had to stop at the stop sign/traffic light. When I started to let up off the clutch, the car started rolling backward. My sister got out of the car and asked the drivers of the cars behind us to please move back so that I would not hit their car. After that experience I was so determined that I learned how to drive my car that day.

Once my "home-girls" and "homeboys" from Union Springs realized I had a car, every Friday evening and Monday morning my car was loaded down with whomever wanted to go home on Friday and back to school on Monday. These were individuals that lived on Campus. Some people were actually sitting in the hatch-back with their feet hanging out while we were going home on Fridays.

Co-op

I did Co-op with the Department of Health and Human Services (Office of Inspector General – Seafarer) in Maryland in the summer of 1980. I was one of 14 students from historically black universities that was selected to participate in the program. Ms. Anita Barney was my Manager and she had me working on ZBB (zero based budgeting). Everyone saw her as this really mean lady, but I really liked her, of course, I was a little afraid of her myself. This was the first time I had flown; and my first flight was to DC the summer of 1980. I always thought that once you fly on a plane, you have "arrived" (status). In the 1980s, they served a meal if the flight was at least an hour flight.

Below is a picture of the students that participated in the Summer Co-op program along with me.

While doing Co-op, I lived with a family in Silver Springs, Maryland. Mrs. Snowden and her daughter Gina rented a room out of their basement to two of us that was in DC for the summer program. Mrs. Snowden had an in-ground pool. An in-ground pool was a status symbol at that time. I remember one weekend, Gina has a pool party, and I was invited to attend since I did not go home. The song, "Upside Down You Turn Me" by Diana Ross was out, and every time I hear that song, I think about that pool party.

Graduation

May 15, 1981, I graduated from Alabama State University as Magna Cum Laude, second in my graduating class. Additionally, I was featured on the "National Registry of Outstanding Graduates" in 1981 and well as was on the Dean's Honor Roll several times during my enrollment at Alabama State University.

I received an offer from United Space Booster in Huntsville, Alabama; Alabama State University Business Office; the Department of Health and Human Services in Washington, DC. and Duke Power in Charlotte, North Carolina. I went on to accept a job at Duke Power Company in the Internal Audit and started to work August 1981. Dewitt Reid was an advisor to Alabama State

University College of Business and had worked out a program with Dean Vaughn where some of the graduates were hired at Duke Power.

First Job after College

While in college, I took a series of accounting classes, (e.g., cost, financial, international, tax, auditing, etc.). Of all the classes I took, I never looked at Auditing as a job or career that I would one day be in. The Jenkins brothers taught the auditing classes. So here I am accepting my first job in Internal Audit with Duke Power. My first supervisor and myself are still friends after 38 years later. I have been working in various areas in Internal Audit for over 38 years domestically and internationally.

> **Motivation:** *Your time is limited, so don't waste it living someone else's life. Don't be trapped by dogma – which is living with the results of other people's thinking. Don't let the noise of others' opinions drown out your own inner voice. And most important, have the courage to follow your heart and intuition. They somehow already know what you truly want to become. Everything else is secondary. (By Steve Jobs)*

I started to work at Duke Power August 1981 in the Internal Audit Department. I was flown from Alabama to Charlotte to interview with four of the audit managers. I was later contacted with an offer from Duke starting at approximately $15,000. I knew I had arrived especially when I compared other offers from United Space Booster in Huntsville, Alabama and Alabama State University Business office. United Space Booster offered me a Pricing Accountant position under $10,000, and ASU much less than United Space Boosters.

At Duke Power Company, we shared phone extensions in 1981. If your phone partner was on the line, you had to wait for them to get off to use the phone. We were on the 7th floor initially and the freight elevator had to be used to get there or we had to take the stairs.

While at Duke, I progressed from an entry level financial Associate Internal Audit to an Internal Auditor, then to a Senior Financial Auditor. I started taking computer classes at CPCC (Central Piedmont Community College) in the mid-1980. After a position came open in the EDP (Electronic Data Processing) Audit group, I applied and was later transferred to the EDP Audit group as an EDP Auditor.

My First Home

At the age of 24, I bought my first home in October 1983 in Charlotte, North Carolina. It was a tri-level, 3 bedrooms, 1 ½ bath, with a basement on Monfreya Court. The interest rate in 1983 was 18%, and the house had negative amortization. To purchase a home at the age of 24 was considered a major milestone in some people's eye. To me, it was the smart thing to do since I was paying rent in an apartment that was not benefitting me. I felt as if I was just giving my money away each month, and I was doing just that. Eight years later and in 1991, I sold this home and moved to Ohio.

Certification

Our Internal Audit department was very competitive. We had certification goals, and these goals were part of our performance evaluation. It seems as if I was always studying for the CPA exam. It was the thing to do because everybody else was. When I was studying for the CPA exam, you had to pass two parts in order to keep the passing parts. If you only pass one part you had to take it over again, if you did not already have two or more parts passed. There were several times where I only passed one of the four parts.

I took the Becker CPA review course, which I really didn't like to format. I also purchased the Gleim CPA Review course books to study for the exam, and I took some of their review courses.

I eventually passed 3 parts of the exam, then I passed the last part the next time around. What a load off my shoulders. I remember my friend Stephanie bringing in a cake to celebrate me passing the exam. I was totally surprised and overjoyed.

Fun Activities

Duke Power was the most fun place I have ever worked. We were very connected as a team. We had annual conference where we got together to do team building.

One memorable activity was an outing on Lake Norman with our then CEO (Bill Lee). Mr. Lee brought his boat and we participated in several water sports such as water skiing and tubing. Of course, I did not participate in any of these. I was on the boat riding. Mr. Lee allowed me to drive the boat for a few minutes. It was rather exciting. I used to wish that I had my own boat to enjoy the peacefulness of the water. I thought that I will have my own yacht one day.

We had talents shows to raise money for United Way. I remember Cedric acting as Ray Charles during one of the talents shows. It was hilarious. We had a committee that would plan activities for each month and or holiday. The Department even took a trip to the beach for one weekend.

During Easter, Stephanie dressed up as a bunny and delivered candy to everyone. We put Valentine candy hearts on everyone's door during Valentine. We dressed in green for St. Patrick's Day and went out to a pub for drink. We had Thanksgiving luncheons and Christmas parties outside of the office. We acknowledge everyone's birthday and had a cake made for them.

We would meet for Happy Hour at some of the local hotels on a regular basis. One hotel that I remember was Adam's Mark Hotel. They serve food and drinks, and during happy hours we could get two drinks for the price of one. They normally had a band most nights and we would dance. As a result of Internal Audit having access to the nuclear facilities, and due to the Nuclear Regulatory Commission (NRC) requirements, the company instituted random drug tests. The weekday visits to these bars ended because we were subject to losing our job if alcohol was found in our blood during a random drug test.

Coal Mines of Virginia and West Virginia

I worked in the coal mines of West Virginia and Virginia. Sometimes, we had to lie flat on our backs on trolley cars that took us five (5) miles into the ground. Our purpose for going into the mines was to confirm the serial number on a piece of mining equipment that is used in calculating depreciation expenses that was being charge to Duke Power Company. There were instances where there were "cave-ins" in another section of the coal mine while we were there in one section. However, we didn't know until we came out that there was a "cave-in".

Of course, you didn't find many blacks working in the coal mines in Virginia and West Virginia. I am sure a lot of the workers were surprised to see a black female at the coal mines. I had to wear coveralls and a hardhat with the light on the front to see while in the mines. We had to bend over or tilt our head to the side in order to walk while in the mine. If I had to use the restroom, I would go around a corner away from the men to handle my business. Black Lung was a prevalent disease among the coal miners. Of course, these companies had set aside a Black Lung fund to support the miner when they got the disease.

I had the opportunity to ride in a helicopter with the mining superintendent while working at one of the mines, along with two other co-workers.

Layoffs

One-year Duke Power announced this major lay-off, and each department had to go through their organization and do an evaluation and determine where they can become more efficient and eliminate resources. They gave the employees the date that the layoff would be announced. So, from the time they told us that there would be layoffs, until the time the layoffs happened, most of the employees did absolutely nothing, no work. We felt that if we would be selected to be laid off, why do any work. After the lay-off day came and passed, everyone got back to work. It ended up that only one person in the Internal Audit department got displaced. He was transferred to another department. So, no one got laid off in our Department.

30th Birthday

I turned 30 on August 8, 1989. I spent my 30th birthday with co-workers at Duke Power Company. The department would normally have a cake made for everyone on their birthday, and my cake had chocolate icing. I remember someone giving me a "pair of thongs" on my birthday. I don't think I ever wore them. They were probably too small.

Hurricane Hugo

In September 1989 Hurricane Hugo hit Charlotte unexpectedly. After the hurricane had passed through, I was looking out of the window the next morning and noticed that a tree had fallen on my 1987 Volvo car. At the time a friend was visiting from out of town and was at my house during the hurricane. I asked him to go and move the tree off my car, and he said that he would not and was afraid to go outside because it was still a little windy. I noticed that one of my neighbors was going up and down the street moving trees and limbs out of the street. He came to my house and pushed the tree off my car. This was the end of that relationship I had with that friend. This was a turning point in my life where I thought that if a man could not make me feel safe, can he be relied upon.

Income During Decade 3

Year	Source	Amount
1980	Alabama State University Business Office	1,245.00
1981	Alabama State University, Duke Power Company	9,653.23
1982	Duke Power Company	19,037.23
1983	Duke Power Company	20,529.69
1984	Duke Power Company	23,424.00
1985	Duke Power Company	26,436.16
1986	Duke Power Company, Red Lobster	30,054.99
1987	Duke Power Company	33,375.45
1988	Duke Power Company, NCNB	37,979.18
1989	Duke Power Company	40,849.31
	Total	**$ 242,584.24**

Motivation: Think Like a Winner

When you change your thinking; You change your belief.

When you change your belief; You change your expectations.

When you change your expectations; You change your attitude.

When you change your attitude; You change your behavior.

Whey you change your behavior; You change your performance.

When you change your performance; You change your life.

(Dr. Walter Doyle Staples)

Investments

In 1990, I wanted to increase my income, so I bought a foreclosed home and remodeled it, and resold the home. I increased my income in that year by 50%. The individuals that I sold the house to was very risky. I set up utilities in my name until they got their finance under control and they didn't pay the bill, and I bought a washing machine that I was never paid for. Nevertheless, that was a risk that I was willing to take at the time.

After 10 years, I left Duke Power in 1991. My friends, family and co-workers thought I was making a big mistake. Duke Power was a very good company to work for, good benefits and pay. Deep down inside of me, I felt that there was something more.

Relocations

- October 1991, I accepted a promotion as a Senior EDP Auditor at Ashland Oil Company in Ashland Kentucky and worked at Ashland for a little over 2 years. I relocated to South Point, Ohio.
- January 1994, I relocated to Greensboro, NC and accepted a promotion as an EDP Audit Supervisor at VF Corporation. My oldest daughter was in College at NCA&T University. I thought it would be cost effective for me to move to Greensboro, NC so that she can stay at home, and I will save on having a mortgage and an apartment rental. I worked at VF for 2 years.
- February 1996, I accepted a promotion as an IT Audit Manager with Sara Lee Hosiery in Winston-Salem, North Carolina. At the time, I lived approximately the same distance from VF Corporation and Sara Lee Hosiery. So, I did not need to relocate, I just drove in the opposite direction.
- While at Sara Lee, I subsequently became the Senior Audit Manager and ran the entire Internal Audit Department which included the financial and information technology audits. After the SLH Internal Audit Department was consolidated with other Internal Audit Departments in Winston-Salem, NC from other Sara Lee divisions, I decided not to transition with the team.
- After the smooth transition of the audit team to the consolidated audit department, I create a new position for myself. I wrote the job description and presented it to the CFO and CEO at the time and emphasized the importance of this position. This was during the Y2K (year 2000), and the date on the computer was supposed to go haywire, and companies might lose all their data, or they may come to a halt. Because of this, companies were putting in new systems and aligning the processes to the new systems.

There was a lot of change happening and I wanted to help drive the change. The position was Director of Business System Process Re-engineering and it was approved. I worked in several capacities while in this role, (e.g., project manager, AR Manager, Logistics Project Team Member, etc.). One of the roles that was most notable during this time was related to the new customer logistics model. The company was changing over from having products on a consignment basis in store to having their customer pay full amount for the products. To transition to the new model, I was part of the team that had to go to the customer's location and explain the new program, as well as show them how much money they owed Sara Lee Hosiery for the consigned products. We then had to work out a payment plan with them. During this time, the team and myself had an opportunity to fly in the Corporate jet to some of the locations. The jet provided seating for approximately 6 people. I used to think that one day I will have my own jet. I worked at Sara Lee Hosiery for six years during 1995 to 2001.

- In February 2001, I relocated to back to Charlotte, North Carolina where I started up Jefferson Wells IT Audit function and worked as an IT Engagement Manager. I worked at Jefferson Wells for only one year. I wanted to become one of their Business Development Manager for the Information Technology area. At the time, I was having to train the Business Development Manager on Information Technology services. So, I thought it would be much easier to train me on becoming a Business Development Manager instead of them learning the "ins" and "outs" about Information Technology, which is not something that you can't just teach to someone overnight. This was not approved by the divisional VP. With me feeling that I had a lot of potential that was not being utilized, I decided to start my own company and provide Information Technology audit services. TITACS Inc. (Thornton Information Technology Auditing and Consulting Services) was created in January 2002.

Second Home

I bought my second home in 1992 where we had a view of the Ohio River. The address was 101 River Drive, South Point, OH. This was a two-story brick home, 4 bedrooms, 3.5 bathrooms, sunroom, with full finished basement, one car garage, balcony on the front with a view of the Ohio River, and an in-ground pool. I decided to live in Ohio because at the time there were no state taxes.

Third Home

I bought my 3rd home in 1995 after moving back to North Carolina from Ohio. The address was 6016 Forest Trails Drive, Winston-Salem, NC. It was a two- story, full brick home with 2 car garage, 4 bedrooms, and 2.5 baths. I lived there until 2001.

40th Birthday

I spend my 40th birthday in the Virgin Islands with two of my friends that also turned 40 that year. We went to St. Thomas, St. John and St. Croix and stay at a resort hotel.

International Travel in this Decade

Location	Date
Brussell, Belgian; Ghent Belgium; Nottingham, England; London, England; Amsterdam, Netherlands	November 29 – December 14, 1994
Kingston , Montego Bay, Ocho Rios (Jamaica)	March 14 – 20, 1998
St. Thomas, St. John, St. Croix (U.S. Virgin Island)	September 1999

Motivation: *When someone say "no", in your head, just say "next". Never give up, persevere.*

When I was working at Duke Power from 1981 to 1991, I always thought that there was something greater that I needed to be doing. I decided I would take an aptitude test to determine where were my strengths and weaknesses. The test was given by the "Employment Security Commission", I think. Nevertheless, I was given a battery of tests including dexterity. When my results came back approximately a few weeks later, the test concluded that I could do anything that I put my mind to. I scored in the upper 90 percentiles in all of the categories that I was tested in.

I was still in the dilemma as to what to do with my life, or what path I should go down. There was something burning in my soul. So, I just started trying different things and pursuing other fields of interest. I have noted some of these below in the Self-improvement and self-actualization section.

Self-Improvement /Self-Actualization

I took golf courses, tennis lessons, and swimming lessons to try and fulfill the potential that I had inside of me. After completing one goal, I was always working on another one.

I studied for and obtained my Certified Information Systems Auditor (CISA) Certification 1990.

I didn't stop in this decade, but it spilled over into the next two decades. There were ballroom dance classes, west coast swing, and shag. All of which gave me temporary satisfaction, but I knew that there was still something much greater and more profound for me. Below are some other career accomplishments.
- I became a real estate salesman in 1989, and subsequently became a Real Estate Broker on April 1, 2006.
- I took the classes to study for and obtain my Life and Health Insurance License February 19, 2003.
- In 2012, I took the pre-requisite classes to obtain my Six Sigma Green Belt certification.
- In 2014, I took a one-week "boot camp" class and subsequently obtained my Project Management Professional (PMP) certification.
- In 2014, I went to a Shoe School in Seattle, Washington and learned how to make a pair of Oxford shoes by hand.

FBI (Federal Bureau of Investigation)

I applied with the FBI to become an undercover agent while working at Duke Power Company. The application process took over a month to complete, and then the background check took forever. I had to document information related to all my immediate family members, and college roommates, places I had worked and the people I worked with.

I then took a written test. Initially they said I failed, then they said I passed. At the time President Reagan was in office. It appears the FBI was trying to increase their minority presence. Later on that year, I was granted an interviewed. I was interviewed by 3 field agents at the same time; one from California, one from DC and one from Charlotte. I had to take an "arms" test to determine how many times I could pull the trigger of a gun in 60 seconds. After it all was said and done, it was indicated that I did not pass the interview, and I couldn't quiet figure that out.

I met a field supervisor several years later that was with the FBI and told him about my experience noted above. He indicated that the reason I was not selected was because I had young children at the time, and there was a chance that years could go by without me seeing them if I became an FBI undercover agent.

Part-time Jobs

- I worked as a waitress at Red Lobster on a part-time basis for several months. The tips were really good. I would come home after the work, and put all my tips on the bed, and my kids would count the money for me. A lot of times, I would bring home at least a $100 in a night.

- North Carolina National Bank (NCNB) used to be one of the primary banks in Charlotte back in the 1980s, before there was Bank of America and Wells Fargo. I worked in their Lock Box processing department at night. My job was to sort checks and put them into these bins, and then key them into the computer so that the funds would be taken from the customer's bank account.

- I worked part-time at the Sears Service Center in Winston-Salem, North Carolina for a few weeks. One day I was on a call with a customer taking their order to have their appliance serviced. We were also instructed to try to sell them some detergent after completing the service order. After the call, the supervisor that was monitoring the call called me into her office to give me an evaluation on how I handled the call. Her concern was that I was not sticking to the script. Based on the questions that the customer was asking me, there was no script for that response, and I answered the question based on my common knowledge. After she gave me her feedback, I politely went back to my work area and got a piece of paper and wrote my resignation letter and dropped the letter off at the front desk on my way out the door. I asked that they send my final check to the address that is shown in the resignation letter. That job was just something to fill some free time that I had. I felt that it was inhibiting my ability to think and use common sense.

One of the main reasons I relocated to Ohio initially was to think. When I was in living in Charlotte, I was involved in so many different things, (e.g. working full time, part-time,

31

refurbishing houses, raising funds for Omega Madigras' Queen, other social activities, etc.). On top of that I had two daughters to rear, one was in high school and the other in junior high school. I felt I needed to slow down and spend time just thinking. In the small town of South Point, Ohio the only thing to do was to go to work, church and to Walmart. I was happy doing just that.

It seems as if I spent more time back in Charlotte attending more events and activities than I did while I was living in Ohio.

In December 1993, I decided to take a position with VF Corporation and moved to Greensboro, North Carolina. The mover had come and packed up the house a few days before me and the kids were to drive to Greensboro, NC. The night before, there was a snowstorm in Ohio. According to the news, the roads were treacherous, and I could not even get out of my neighborhood. So, we ended getting a train ticket to go to Greensboro, North Carolina.

We could not stay in the house because I had the power cut-off as of the date we had planned to leave. I left my Volvo in the garage and planned to fly back a few days later to get it once the roads had cleared up. We called a taxi to take us to the train station.

The train trip was unforgettable. Somewhere out in the middle of Manassas, Virginia, the train stopped on the tracks. We were stranded there with no heat or food. Amtrak had to fly in engineers to repair the train after several hours of being on the track. There was no backup train to come get us. Once the train was repaired, we then had to wait at another train station for hours until a train came to take us on to Greensboro, North Carolina. I vowed that I would never ride an Amtrak train again.

Approximately, 20 years later I did take a trip from Charlotte to Washington, DC on Amtrak to visit the Martin Luther King Memorial located in West Potomac Park next to the National Mall.

Income During Decade 4

Year	Source	Amount
1990	Duke Power Company	44,061.15
1991	Duke Power Company, Ashland Oil, Real Estate Investment	61,563.15
1992	Ashland Oil Company	48,632.04
1993	Ashland Oil Company	57,532.83
1994	VF Corporation	61,577.88
1995	VF Corporation	60,060.15
1996	VF Corporation, Sara Lee Hosiery, Sears Service Center	64,726.64
1997	Sara Lee Hosiery	68,488.44
1998	Sara Lee Hosiery	73,521.82
1999	Sara Lee Hosiery	86,719.97
	Total	**$ 626,884.07**

Motivation: *Don't try to be what you are not.*

When I was in Junior High School, the boys in the neighborhood would come to our house during the summer months. We would sit out in the yard and talk and play games. All the guys were trying to get them a big afro. Whenever you "corn-row" or braid a person's hair, it causes it to grow faster. I would "corn-row" their hair and charge $0.50. Fifty cents could buy five (5) or more candy bars, a gallon of gas, five (5) cokes, a loaf of bread, or etc.

I took Home Economics in the 9th grade where I learned how to sew. When I went to High School, I would make my clothing because my Mother could not afford to buy us new clothing on a regular basis. I was a bridesmaid in Kathy's wedding and I made my bridesmaid dress.

I even made a dress for an acquaintance and charged her $15, and that was a lot of money in 1975-76. When I went to college, my roommate Donna pledge the Alpha Kappa Alpha sorority (AKA). They had to have a specific outfit made for their "cross-over" ceremony, and I made the outfit for my roommate.

When I started my job at Sara Lee Hosiery in 1996, they had a lay-off my first day on the job. One of the employees that was laid off in the Internal Audit Department came to me crying wondering why they laid her off and hired me on the same day. I had no answer to that question because I was just as shocked as she was. However, our positions were totally different. Every year thereafter, Sara Lee Hosiery had a planned lay-off. They would split the company up into two divisions one year, and then put it back together the next year. Thus, I saw that this was not a very stable company, and figured I needed to work on a plan for my future stability. I worked on my business plan for five years prior to me incorporating in 2001. Of course, Sara Lee Hosiery and the other local divisions were eventually combined into Hanes Brand and were spun off as a separate company from Sara Lee Corporation, and is currently listed separately on the NYSE.

Mentee'

During my tenure at Sara Lee Hosiery, I became the mentee' to the Chief Information Officer (CIO).   Over the years, our friendship has flourished, and she is still a person that I have the upmost respect and admiration for. Because of her, I was exposed to a lot of professional organizations, such as Jack and Jill of America which is an African American organization that creates a medium of contact for children which will stimulate growth, and development and provide constructive educational, cultural, civic, health, recreational and social programs. The members of this organization are professional women who are doctors, lawyers, business executives, professors, teachers, etc.

During October 3-8, 2000, she made it possible for me to attend the National Black MBA Association annual conference in Chicago, Illinois. That years their theme was, "Harvesting the Fruit of our Roots in the Diaspora". There was another organization called the Information Technology Forum, that included the top black Information Technology professional around the country, and I had the pleasure of attending the forum with her one year and listening to great minds.

TITACS, Inc.

2002: On January 1, 2002, I started my own consulting company, TITACS Inc. (Thornton Information Technology Auditing and Consulting Services.) My first contract was March 2002 with Sara Lee. The person that hired me had previously worked for me when I was the IT Audit Manager at Sara Lee Hosiery.

2008: During this time, I also attempted to start a company with my family members. This included my daughters, sons-in-law, nieces, nephews, etc. (the younger generation). We had our first meeting in December 2008, in Montgomery, Alabama. I had everyone sign the Confidentially Agreement. I created an organization chart; and assigned roles and responsibilities. The first task for everyone was to learn a foreign language and try to visit a manufacturing plant in the upcoming months.

I created a status report so that everyone would report monthly on the progress they were making toward their new language. I bought each person the CD for the language of their choice along with the related books (e.g., French, German, Spanish, Italian, Arabic, etc.). After 2 months, I concluded that since a status report could not be provided to me monthly, my level of confidence was reduced in that I did not think they were ready for what I was proposing at the time. So, the initiative was pretty much dissolved for lack of enthusiasm and interest. Of course, at the time there was a lot going on in everyone's life such as a recent marriage, new jobs, school, etc.

Heaven's Highway, Inc.

2015: Seven years later, January 2, 2015, I set-up Heaven's Highway, Inc. (HHI) for the product development and manufacturing aspect of a company I was trying to start in 2008. I created my first proposal in April 2018 to provide services under HHI, and it was signed and accepted.

Fourth Home

During July 2003, I bought my 4th home at 2135 Light Brigade Drive, Matthews, NC 28105. It was a two-story home with full finished basement, 5 bedroom, 4 baths, 2 offices, 2 dens, living, dining, exercise room, and an enclosed inground pool. During October 2019, I sold my home and moved into an apartment temporarily.

50th Birthday

I celebrated my 50th birthday in Honolulu, Hawaii in 2009. I stayed at the Hilton Resort on the beach in Honolulu for a week. I had the opportunity to partake in the festivities and cultures of the Island.

International Travel in this Decade

Location	Date
Kuwait, Kuwait	May 6, 2001 – June 7, 2001
Cairo, Egypt	May 6, 2001 – June 7, 2001
Frankford, Germany	May 6, 2001 – June 7, 2001
Bahrain (Persian Gulf)	May 6, 2001 – June 7, 2001
Abu Dhabi, UAE	May 6, 2001 – June 7, 2001
Paris, France	June 8, 2002 – June 22, 2002
Copenhagen, Denmark	September 7, 2002 – September 21, 2002
Oslo, Norway	September 7, 2002 – September 21, 2002
Antwerp, Belgium	September 7, 2002 – September 21, 2002
Lisbon, Portugal	September 7, 2002 – September 21, 2002
The Rock of Gibraltar, UK	September 7, 2002 – September 21, 2002
Florence, Italy	September 7, 2002 – September 21, 2002
Pisa, Italy	September 7, 2002 – September 21, 2002
Rome, Italy	September 7, 2002 – September 21, 2002
Vigo Spain	September 7, 2002 – September 21, 2002
Barcelona, Spain	September 7, 2002 – September 21, 2002
Paris, France	September 7, 2002 – September 21, 2002
Canterbury, England (Dover)	September 7, 2002 – September 21, 2002
Monte Carlo, Monaco	September 7, 2002 – September 21, 2002
San Juan, Puerto Rico	February 8, 2004 – February 20., 2004
Barbados	September 25, 2004 – October 2, 2004
Montreal, Canada	September 7, 2005 – September 11, 2005
Barbados	September 24, 2005 – October 1, 2005
Montreal, Canada	July 9, 2006 – July 14, 2006
Israel (Jerusalem, Bethlehem, Caesarea, Tiberias, Sea of Galilee, Sepphoris, Capernaum, Jordan, Mount of the Beatitudes, Haifa)	August 19, 2007 – August 27, 2007

Motivation: *Set specific goals and objectives for your dreams and take action.*

During this decade, I grossed $1 million in income. At the beginning of this decade, I made some major changes in my life.

I started up my own consulting company in 2002, TITACS Inc. (Thornton Information Technology Auditing and Consulting Services) and got my first contract with Sara Lee. After that, I worked on a contract basis with Resources Global, Mobius Search, Sherpa, Dassault Systemes (France), Solidworks, Enovia, Matrix-One, Delmia, Simulia, Novant Health, Jefferson Wells, etc.

In the Zone

I was working at Wachovia Bank in 2003, and on October 29, 2003 as I was on my way to the food court, someone asked me if I wanted to take a chance on guessing the number of pieces of candy that was in this huge cake plate for a $1.00. I said why not, they were raising funds for United Way. So, I was supposed to guess a number and write it on the back of the ticket along with my name and phone number. I guessed that there were 213 pieces of candy in that cake plate. A few days later, I was contacted indicating that I had guessed the exact number of pieces. Of course, I won $25, the cake plate and all the candy that was in it, because I had guessed the exact number of pieces. I shared the candy with the entire Internal Audit Department.

> 8/29/04: As I was closing the blinds in my house, I thought about calling Betty and asking if they wanted to use my house for a cook-out. When I called her, she asked me that question?
>
> 8/30/04: When setting the alarm to my house this morning before going to work, the thought of my alarm going off crossed my mind. At 8:13am, CPI called about my alarm going off.

Synchronicity/Blessings
> 12/5/03: I won the grand price in a raffle to help less fortunate families, which was a $100 gift certificate to the Palms Restaurant.
> 12/17/03: I was attending a dinner with a friend to celebrate another friend's birthday, and one of the friends picked up the check for me and the birthday person at Jack Mason.
> 12/18/03: I unexpectedly received a Christmas gift from two co-workers while working on a contract assignment.
> 12/25/03: The Smith family (next door neighbors) prepared a dessert plate for me. This was the first Christmas in my new house.
> 01/02/04: I received a $500 bonus referral check from Resource Global.

01/07/04: I was a member of this organization whose goal was to carry-on the legacy of the organization to young children. A friend that was also a member knew that I did not eat meat at the time, prepared a large container of vegetable soup for me.

01/09/04: A check came in the mail unexpectedly from Blue Cross Blue Shield for $284.

04/09/04: The Towing Company gave me a free tow because they were late ($65)

08/26/04: While turning left into Tai Pai Express for lunch, the man I was dating at the time passed by me as I was turning. At another time, as I was merging onto to I-85 North from the left, he was also merging onto I-85 North from the right.

Income During Decade 5

Year	Source	Amount
2000	Sara Lee Hosiery	101,719.72
2001	Sara Lee Hosiery, Jefferson Wells	135,682.70
2002	Jefferson Wells, TITACS	103,362.30
2003	TITACS, Contracts	100,372.25
2004	TITACS, Contracts	81,797.33
2005	TITACS, Contracts	174,326.43
2006	TITACS	76,361.55
2007	TITACS	130,481.95
2008	TITACS	52,577.18
2009	TITACS	56,351.38
	Total	**$ 1,013,032.79**

Motivation: *Wealth is of the mind. Build ideas of wealth and abundance in your mind. The feeling of wealth produces wealth. Subconscious is never short of ideas. Your wealth is dependent on your subconscious mind.*

Decade 6: Age 51-60 *(2010 – 2019)*
Chapter 10 – Living the Life I Want

Oprah's The Life You Want Weekend in Atlanta, GA

During September 5–6, 2014**,** Oprah indicated that she wanted us all to fulfill our greatest potential, and to find our calling and summon the courage to live it. Oprah's masterminds were a part of this event: Deepak Chopra, Elizabeth Gilbert, Rob Bell, and Iyanla Vanzant.

This weekend was focused on "what have I been called to do?" I worked on creating the highest, grandest vision for my life, and to have every step I take to move me in that direction. We were instructed to pay attention to the whispers. We went through an exercise of "Seeing our life today".

This exercise required us to rank the following by importance to us; and then we had to assign a happy or sad face based on how we felt about each. Here are my rankings:
1. Spirituality/faith/belief – good ☺
2. Body/health/well-being -bad ☹
3. Financial situation -so-so ☺
4. Spouse/mate/partner – so – so ☺
5. Family/children/grandchildren/parents – good ☺
6. Contributions to the world – bad ☹
7. Home – good ☺
8. Occupation – so-so ☺
9. Friendships – good ☺
10. Travel – bad ☹
11. Fun – good ☺
12. Hobbies and Passions – bad ☹

On 9/6/14, I wrote that a year from this date, "I want to see my successful company and life and love partner come to fruition and flourish, (Heaven's Highway, Inc.). "

In January 2015, I started up Heaven's Highway, Inc. A friend gave me a Ford truck, and the personalized tag read, "Heavens". I later transferred that tag to my 1987 Volvo and then to my 2019 Volvo S90, which is currently the company car for Heaven's Highway, Inc.

Additionally, during this weekend of the Oprah Tour, we also created a new vision. Here is my new vision:
1. I'm on the way
2. I feel energized
3. I have a mission
4. I choose happiness

5. I am positive
6. I can do this
7. I'm compassionate
8. I love myself
9. I'm in charge of me
10. I am present
11. I am successful
12. I put me first
13. I'm Making good choices
14. I'm ready
15. I am connected to life
16. I trust myself
17. I listen to my heart
18. I'm Blessed
19. I'm happy
20. I can change
21. I'm taking steps to be healthier
22. I am getting back to my ideal weight of 145
23. I'm beautiful
24. I'm loving my body more and more
25. I speak gently to myself
26. I look forward
27. I won't be taken for granted
28. I am powerful
29. I will be all that I can be
30. I am becoming a billionaire
31. I am connected to all there is
32. My heart is open
33. I love ME
34. I matter
35. I can do anything
36. I have what I need, I just need to use it
37. I know my life has meaning

Below is my "My New Vision Statement"

I wish for a more intimate relationship with God. I want a successful multi-billion international business to pass on to family members (Heaven Highway, Inc.). I want a healthy body and lifestyle. I want to travel at any moments' notice in my own private plane or Lear jet. I want a life partner for personal and business relationships. I want to be debt free as well as help my children and immediate family to become debt free. I want to have an international impact on the world. I want to show God's love to everyone that comes in contact with me. I want my business to provide products to enrich, simplify, and add comfort to a person's life. I want a beautiful home on the ocean, river or lake. I want to help people improve their lives. I want to obtain patents (design/utility) for all the product ideas I have. I want to start in the US first, "state by state", then go international. I want a Lamborghini.

Oprah indicated that *"With every experience, you alone are painting your own canvas – though by though, choice by choice."*

Elizabeth Gilbert said, *"In order to be what you want to be, stop being what you are. It is best to live your own life imperfectly; than to live an imitation of a perfect live."*

You are the "I AM" that I am
1. I am asserting the mastery of my real self
2. I am using my will power
3. I am alive
4. I am successful
5. I am beautiful
6. I am an eloquent speaker
7. I am debt free
8. I am loved
9. I am in the perfect personal relationship
10. I am wealthy
11. I am rich
12. I am at my ideal weight
13. I am blessed
14. I am well able
15. I am victorious
16. I am creative
17. I am wise
18. I am healthy
19. I am in shape
20. I am energetic
21. I am happy
22. I am positive
23. I am passionate
24. I am strong
25. I am confident
26. I am secure
27. I am attractive
28. I am valuable

29. I am redeemed
30. I am forgiven
31. I am anointed
32. I am accepted
33. I am approved
34. I am prepared
35. I am qualified
36. I am motivated
37. I am focused
38. I am disciplined
39. I am determined
40. I am patient
41. I am kind
42. I am generous
43. I am excellent
44. I am equipped
45. I am empowered
46. I am prosperous
47. I am a child of the "Most High God"

Thoughts are Powerful and Becomes Thing

September 24, 2016 (Saturday) – I had been trying to get my pressure washer started this morning. I eventually called my son-in-law and asked if he would come over to crank the pressure washer.   He eventually arrived approximately an hour later, and we did various things to try to get it cranked, such as replaced spark plug, let some of the old gas out of tank, ensure oil level was ok, etc. So eventually it cranked, and I immediately went to work pressure washing the steps on the front of my house. After a few minutes, the pressure washer ran out of gas, and cut off. I filled it back up with gas and tried to re-crank it. After 15-30 minutes of trying to crank it, I gave up and called my son-in-law and asked him to come back by the house on Sunday after he gets off work.

In the meantime, I was thinking that I should go ahead and wash my hair for Sunday and try to catch the movie, "The Magnificent Seven" with Denzel Washington that had just come out on Friday. I was also thinking that I should have my hair ready in the event I go to the Panther game, which was on Sunday also. I washed my hair and was able to catch the 7:00pm movie. After leaving the movie, I turned my phone on and I had a message from Laverne asking if I wanted to go the Panther game on Sunday. She had a free ticket and of course, I was elated.

September 25, 2016 (Sunday) – In the process of getting my clothes ready for the game on Sunday, I realized that I did not have a short sleeve Panthers' shirt or top. So, I just put my long sleeve Panthers' shirt in the back seat of my car. I went downtown to tailgate with the Team and other acquaintances. I was admiring everyone's short sleeve Panthers' shirts, and I indicated that I wanted a short sleeve Panthers' top. During the game, t-shirts were being thrown to individuals in stands. I was in section 514, and we sometimes assume that since we are so high up, we never get any of the goodies. I was reading something in the program booklet and looked up and there was a t-shirt coming my way. I immediately grabbed it along with the guy that was sitting directly in front of me. So, I released the shirt so that he could have it. Then he turned around and gave it to me. It was a short sleeve Panthers' shirt.

September 27, 2016 (Tuesday)– I was driving to work thinking about the conversation I had the previous day with co-worker regarding the Audit Director coming to the CIC facility for the day. He was bringing the new Senior Audit Manager onsite to meet some of the employees. My co-worker indicated that she did not know what time they would be arriving as they were coming from Phoenix Arizona and Minnesota. She thought that maybe she might not have arrived for work by the time the Audit Director and the Senior Audit Manager arrives, but just wanted to put me on notice.

I am normally an early arrival to work, around 7am. So, as I was driving, I was thinking to myself that I hope I am the first one to meet them when they arrive. So, as the day progressed, I was focused on completing my work. So around 11:20am, I decided that I would do my normal walk during the lunch hour, and then go to the cafeteria to get me something to eat during my walk. As I was traveling my normal route during the lunch hour, I would enter this hallway in Building 1 that was behind the computer center and it dead ends eventually. As I was beginning to turn around at the dead end, I noticed two gentlemen with "red" paper badges on their jacket. I looked up and it was the Director and Senior Audit Manager. They had taken a wrong turn and ended up at this dead end. It appeared that the Director was on the phone calling someone to come and get them. I immediately recognized him and had assumed it was Senior Audit Manager based on his profile that I had read earlier that morning. I introduced myself and told them that the Holy Spirit had sent me to come get them. I then escorted them to the Audit Department offices which was in building 3. I was the first person in the Internal Audit department to meet them.

October 26, 2016 (Wednesday) – I called West today to see if we were still on for him coming by my house on Thursday to start the repair work. When he answered the phone, he indicated that he was just talking about me and said that he needed to call me to see if he was still on for Thursday. Donald, one of his workers confirmed that they were just having that conversation.

Sunday, February 5, 2017: While in Church today, I was trying to get Michael's attention before the service started, so that I could get his phone number for a friend of mine. I was sitting on the outer aisle up against the wall on the left-hand side of the church. Michael, who is an usher was working the next aisle over going towards the center of the church. He was walking up and down that aisle greeting the members and visitors. I continued to try and make eye contact, but he never looked in my direction. So, I said in my mind, "Michael, come over here", and then I forgot about it.   Approximately, 5 minutes later the service started. The first 10 – 15 minutes of the service was focused on the up-coming mission trips. After that the choir started the praise and worship part of the service, I was standing up singing, and I looked to my left and there Michael was standing right beside me. I asked for his number, and he gave me his business card and wrote his mobile number on the back.

I was watching the LI (51st) Super Bowl tonight, with Atlanta Falcons playing the New England Patriot. The score was 28-3 is the latter part of the third quarter with Atlanta leading. It was after 9:00 pm, so I decided to go to bed since it appeared that Atlanta had won already. I said to myself that it would be great to wake up Monday morning and hear that the New England Patriots had come back and beat Atlanta. One of the reasons I was thinking this is that some of the Atlanta fans had been giving the Panthers' fan a hard time about going to the Super Bowl in 2016, and not coming back with a victory. Sure enough, as I am checking my email on the Monday morning (February 6, 2017) following the Super Bowl, one of the job-related emails indicated that New England came back to win the game in overtime.

Tuesday, April 10, 2018: I was at the gym working out today. It was passed the regular lunch hour and I was thinking about what I wanted to eat for lunch. I was thinking about going to K&W Cafeteria not far from the gym. I wanted green beans, cabbage, spinach with boiled egg and Mexican corn bread. When I got to the restaurant, it was closed to 2pm. As I was going through the cafeteria style restaurant line, I noticed that there was one serving of spinach left. I was hoping the person ahead of me did not get the spinach. So, when it was my time to order, I got the last serving. Then when I got to the container with the cabbage, the server said that it only had juice. I asked her to get a spoon to see if there were enough cabbage for a serving, and it was when using the spoon to scoop them out. There were plenty green beans. The Mexican cornbread was cooked crisp just as I like it. This may not seem as significant but note that the vegetables that are served each day are different. But today, I really wanted the above vegetables, and the universe provided those for me.

Friday, October 4, 2019: Today, I didn't bring my lunch, so I went to the cafeteria at the company I was working and got me a salad. There are tables outside of the cafeteria and a waterfall. I decided I would go outside and eat my lunch under one of the tables that had an umbrella covering it. I got one of the tables that were close to a tree. After eating my lunch, I was sitting there staring at the tree, and there was a small green lizard crawling down the tree. I closed my eyes for a few minutes to try and get me a "cat nap". Then I looked up to ensure my head was covered by the umbrella in the event a snake fell from the tree. A few minutes later I was looking at the same tree the green lizard was on, and there was a snake crawling down the tree. I ran inside the cafeteria.

Friday, October 11, 2019: While driving to work this morning around 6:20am on Taylor Road, the road was dark, so I turned my headlights on the high beam. I was thinking that with my lights being on bright, some deer may run across the road because of the lights. Then I thought that since this street had a lot of office buildings, deer are probably not out here. Within the next minute, I made a left onto Senator Royale Street, and there was a deer on the side of the road staring at me. I said, Jesus!! Then I had another thought, that since the deer manifested that quick; someone would come and view my house today and make me an offer since I had no "Showings" during the week. At 11:28am, I received a text requesting a showing of my house for 1:45pm today.

Monday, November 11, 2019: I was in the restroom shortly after lunch today, and I was thinking that I needed to say something about my work status to one of the Managing Directors. I said to myself or thought that he will come to my desk and I mention it then. At approximately 2:00pm, I was hard at work and someone called my name. I turned around and it was the Managing Director along with wife and two children standing outside of my cubicle. So, he introduced his family to me, and we chatted for a while. Someone made the comment about hoping to see me later. This is the point where I mentioned to him that I was winding down on my work on the current project, and wanted to know if there was something else they wanted me to do before I "jetted-out". He said that I am sure we have plenty of additional work for you to do.

Letting Go

I was at a point in my life where I felt I wasn't progressing. I had a very full schedule, and was doing a lot of things, but at the end of the day I did not see any progress. When I use the word progress, I mean personal and professional growth, increase in my wealth, satisfying and stimulating personal relationships. I began to take a look at the things that were taking up my time but were not really contributing to some of my goals. During this decade, I made some hard decisions and some of these are noted below:
- December 2012, I ended my part-time work with CW Williams. I was not being paid on time or at all. However, I felt I should do whatever I could to help the organization out since it serviced an underprivileged community.
- February 22, 2013, I ended my two-year employment with CHS as an employee. I had no desire for long-term employment because I owned my own company. Providing contracting services at CHS was not an option when I accepted the job. By working there as an employee, I was not benefitting from being an officer of my company.
- December 2014, I ended my contract position with IBC in Philadelphia, PA after working there approximately 2 years. I had an apartment on Broad Street, and I would take the subway to Market Street to work every day. I traveled back and forth to Charlotte, NC every week. I never knew if the plane would leave on time to take me back to Charlotte

or if the flight would be canceled. I grew tired of spending so much time in the airport in Philadelphia.

- December 2015, a personal relationship I had been in ended after approximately 6 years. We did not have the same goals and aspirations.
- January 2017, I decided to let go of my role in this tax-exempt organization. I was over the Audit and Finance Committee, and over the past year or so, my participation in activities and meetings had dwindled due to my work travel schedule. I felt that I was not truly engaged and thought it was in the best interest of the organization for someone else to have that role.
- October 2019, I sold and closed on my house. I wanted a different lifestyle. I grew tired of the mowing of my lawn and raking leaves during the spring, summer and fall months. When I traveled, my weekends would be spent working in my yard. I wanted more time to complete this book, focus on my true calling in this life by listening to the still voice within me. I wanted to eliminate all the routine tasks that were taking up my time.

Suggestion on How to Live a Happy and Rewarding Life

- Take time to smell the roses
- Take a nap on Sunday afternoon
- Drink 8 glasses of water a day
- Never deprive someone of hope. It might be all they have
- Be thankful for every meal
- Don't be afraid to say I am sorry
- Don't take good health for granted
- Don't interrupt
- Don't tailgate
- Improve your performance by improving your attitude
- Wave at children on the school bus
- Listen to your children
- Leave everything a little better than you found it
- Leave the toilet seat in the down position
- Keep it simple
- Keep good company
- Keep your promise
- Be kinder than necessary
- Take good care of those you love
- Make a habit to do nice things for people who will never find out
- Wear outrageous underwear under the most formal business attire
- Vote
- Judge success by the degree that you are enjoying peace, health and love

- Be a good loser
- Be a good winner
- Be romantic
- Live so that when your children think of fairness, caring and integrity, they think of you
- Enjoy real maple syrup
- Never refuse homemade brownies
- Never give anyone a fruitcake
- Remember other people's birthday
- Sing in the shower
- Don't nag
- Don't gossip
- Don't expect money to bring you happiness
- Be forgiving of yourself and others
- Never give up on anyone. Miracles happen everyday
- Say "thank you" a lot
- Take a dog to obedience school. You'll both learn a lot
- Slow Dance
- Don't rain on other people's parades
- Don't postpone joy
- Stop blaming others. Take responsibility for every area of your life
- Take care of your reputation. It is your most valuable asset
- Count your blessings
- Whistle
- Marry only for love
- Call your Mother
- Do more than is expected
- Be there when people need you
- Be someone's hero
- Support your community. Support it generously with your time and money

60th Birthday

I went to the Kentucky Derby this year with a friend of mine to celebrate my birthday. We were dressed in our hats and fine attire. We attended the annual parade and participated in various activities (e.g., boat ride down the Ohio River, outdoor concerts, parties, clubs, etc.). A local family hosted us for dinner one evening. The food was delicious (e.g., ribs, collard green, yams, potato salad, macaroni and cheese, homemade pies, corn bread, green salad, tea, etc.)

International Travel this Decade

Location	Date
Jamaica	February 2014
Cayman Island (British Overseas Island)	Cruise – May 2014
Cozumel, Mexico	Cruise – May 2014
Montego Bay, Jamaica	Cruise – May 2014
Aruba	September 2014
Toronto, Canada	August 2017, November 2017
Toronto, Canada	August 2018, November 2018

Motivation: *Live in the feeling of being what you want to be.*
If you would like to accomplish something, you must expect to complete it for yourself.

Money Comes Your Way Everyday, One Way or Another

I have always looked down when I walked. When we were young, we would go looking for money in the yard of our house. We were told that our great grandmother buried money in the back yard. If we found a penny, we would rejoice, because a penny could get us two pieces of bubble gum, or two cookies at Mr. George's store.

A penny and a nickel went a long way back in the 60s and 70s. You could buy a candy bar for a nickel; "Now and Later" candy for a penny; a coke for a dime; and gas was fifty cents a gallon, etc.

Recycling

We would also look for empty bottles that had been thrown along the side of the road to return to the general store to get the deposit on the bottle. The deposit ranged from $.01 to $.05. Returning bottles to the store for a deposit was the first phase of what we refer to today as "recycling".

Mr. George and Edna Smith had a neighborhood store. This store maintained the basics that any family may need such as flour, sugar, bread, grits, milk, candy, etc. Mr. George would only open the store when you would come to buy something. I remember he had these bad dogs in his yard, and we would not come inside his fence unless he called the dogs back.

A Penny a Day

September 14, 2016: I had been listening to a video about manifesting money. The person in the video said to try this exercise by just focusing on a penny. So, as I am walking behind this lady to the cafeteria, a penny fell out of her hand. Of course, she picked it up. After this, I started to really pay attention to manifesting money.

September 15, 2016: I was doing my morning walk at work. I usually get to work around 6:00am and spend an hour walking through the buildings. As I was walking down the hallway, I saw a dime that was stuck under a pipe.

Friday, October 14, 2016: I parked in the Walmart parking lot on Sardis Road. When I got out of my car, there were two quarters, a dime, a nickel and two pennies on the ground right beside my car.

Saturday, October 15, 2016: I called the Manager at Lowe's and discussed the ordeal I had been going through with the repair of my pressure washer. He told me that they would be giving me credit for a new pressure washer since mine could not be repaired. I went into the store this morning and got a new pressure washer.

Tuesday, October 18, 2016: As I was entering the turn-stall at work after scanning my badge to enter the building, I noticed a penny in the turn-stall. I did not pick it up because I may have gotten jammed or caught in the turn-stall as it is supposed to continue to turn.

Wednesday, October 19, 2016: I stopped at the QT Gas Station on Monroe Road to fill my BMW up with gas that afternoon. I got the windshield washer brush and proceeded to clear my front windshield; I notice a penny in front of my car on the ground.

Immediately after that, a man came by and asked if I had a dollar, so he could put some gas in his car. I told him I did not have any cash. After I finished with the windshield and filling my car up with gas, something in my spirit told me to look in my cigarette tray and give him whatever change I had, so I did. After going over giving him the change, I look to see what he was doing, and I am sure it was not enough to even put a gallon of gas in his vehicle. So, I went over and asked him how he got to the gas station if he ran out of gas. He said he barely made there. So, I decided to put $5.00 worth of gas on my credit card into his vehicle.

Thursday, October 20, 2016: I checked my answering machine at home today and had a message from Lowe's indicating that since my pressure washer could not be fixed and that I can come and get my refund of $106.15 for the repair cost.

Friday, October 21, 2016: After getting off from work around 1:30 p.m., I decided to go the movies to see "The Accountant" with Ben Affleck and "Jack Reacher" with Tom Cruise. I was the second person waiting in line at the concession stand. When the lady in front of me moved to the counter, I notice there was a shiny penny on the floor in front of me where she was standing. I picked up the penny and said thank you Jesus for his continued blessing. I went to the counter and ordered a small bag of popcorn. The small bag was $5.99. After seeing how small the bag was, I asked to cashier to give me a medium bag which was $6.99. The cashier had to call another cashier to find out how to credit out the money I paid for the small bag and charge me for the medium bag. The other cashier told her to just go ahead and give me a medium bag of popcorn. This resulted in $1.00 savings. After leaving the movies, I went to Walmart to return a stadium chair that a friend had given me for my birthday. I was planning to take the chair to the Magic City Classic in Birmingham the weekend of October 29th, 2016. Legion Field instituted a new bag policy, and the type chair I had was no longer allowed. I was refunded approximately $21.29. On the way out the door, I found another penny and a dime on the floor. I said, "Thank you Jesus for blessing me".

Saturday, October 22, 2016: I spend the whole day at home, and pressure washed my driveway. I stopped around 6:00pm. I wore a blue pair of jogging pants while pressuring washing the driveway. These were the same pair of pants that I had worn the previous

Saturday while I was pressuring washing my walkway. When I work in my yard, I usually take off my dirty and wet clothing in the garage before coming into the house. I always empty my pocket because sometimes I have tissue in them to clean my face and nose. This pair of jogging pants were in the dryer from where I had washed them earlier in the week. So, as I was emptying my pocket, there was a penny in the pocket.

Sunday, October 23, 2016: After leaving Church today, I went to Walmart to buy groceries for the week. As I entered the door, I looked to the right into the McDonald's Restaurant and noticed a penny on the floor in front of the counter. I decided to go do my shopping because there were people in McDonald's being waited on by the Cashier. After I had checked out at the cash register, I headed back towards the McDonald's to see if the penny was still there. Surely it was. I went into McDonald's and picked up the penny and preceded out the door.

I went to Dollar Tree to purchases a sympathy card for two friends that had a death in their family. I was on my way to the "Wake" when I stopped by Dollar Tree. As I was entering the store, I glanced back to the parking lot, and there was a motorcycle that was parked near the entrance, and there was a penny in front of the motorcycle.

Monday, October 24, 2016: This morning around 8:00 am I went to the Food Court in the building I was working in to get my usual breakfast (e.g, English Muffin, Boiled egg, Grape jelly). While I was at the register to the right, I noticed a dime that was under the table near the register to the left. After paying for my food, I politely moved to the other side and picked up the dime under the table. Today, I am graduating from a penny to a dime. Later on today, I received an email from the Security Awareness team informing me that I have been randomly selected to receive a gift for participating in the Security Day which was on October 13, 2016.

On my way home from work, I took a different route because the traffic was so congested while trying to get on I-485. As I am driving down Sugar Creek Road, the traffic had slowed down and came to a stop, I look out of my window on the ground and noticed that there were three (3) pennies beside my car in the middle of the road. I didn't get out to get them because I thought that the traffic would suddenly start to move, and the person behind me would become agitated with me.

Friday, October 28, 2016: We were on our way to Birmingham, Alabama to the Magic City Classic and decided to stop somewhere in South Carolina so we could get something to eat and everyone could use the restroom. My daughters, grandkids and son-in-law were with me. We stopped at a Subway off I-85 South. As I stepped out of the van, there was a dime in the parking lot right beside our vehicle.

Saturday, October 29, 2016: We went to Legion Field early this morning to set-up everything to tailgate. On my way from the porta-john, I found a penny in the gravel lot. We were at Legion Field from approximately 6:00am to 8:00pm. We also went to the football game between Alabama State University and Alabama A & M. Later on during the day, I was walking around the tailgate area getting my 10,000 steps in, and I found two (2) more pennies. Each time I said, "Thank you Jesus for blessing me".

Sunday, October 30, 2016: We left Residence Inn in Birmingham around 6:00 am heading back to Charlotte, North Carolina. I had planned to fill the van up with gas the night before but was too tired to stop on the way back to the hotel from the game. So, we stopped at the Chevron which was down the street from the hotel to gas up the vehicle. I got out and filled the tank. A receipt did not print at the pump, so I had to go into the store to get a receipt. It really irritates me when I must go inside to get a receipt. My shoes were untied, so when I got in the store to the counter to get the receipt, I bent down to tie my shoes, and there was a penny on the floor right in front of my shoe.

After getting back to Charlotte today, I decided to go and "Vote Early". I waited in line approximately 45 minutes. After I voted, I went to the nearby Walmart off Sardis and Monroe Road to buy me some muscadines grapes. As I was exiting Walmart, there was a penny on the outside of the entrance door.

Tuesday, November 1, 2016: I didn't sleep very well last night. I was up at 4:30am. I decided to get the clothes out of the dryer that I had put in before going to bed the night before, and a penny fell out of my clothes dryer. I said thank you Jesus.
Later this morning as I was walking through the cafeteria doing my 6:00 am morning walk, a penny was on top of one of the tables. I said, "Thank you Jesus for your blessings".

Thursday, November 3, 2016: While standing in line at the Food Court to pay for my breakfast of $1.37 (English muffin, boiled egg), there was a dime in front of me near the cash register on the floor. This is the same cash register where I found a dime on October 24.

Friday, November 4, 2016: While listening to "Master Key to Wealth" by Joseph Murphy, as I was doing my morning walk that usually starts at 6:00am; I decided to walk through the food court today. At the entrance to the food court from outside, there was a shiny penny near the door. As I continued through the training center, which was off from the food court, I found another penny. I walked the same area in the training area for three time. I found a third penny as I was walking through the Training area, (The pennies were dated 1982, 2004, 2016). I said, "Thank You Jesus for your continued blessings".

Tuesday, November 8, 2016: (Election Day) When I arrive to work this morning around 5:30am, I started to scan my badge to go through the turn-stall, and noticed a penny at the entrance to the turn-stall.

I dropped off my purse at my desk and put my lunch in the refrigerator. I then proceeded to walk towards the cafeteria as part of my morning walk. As I was walking among the tables in the cafeteria, there on top of one of the tables were a nickel, dime and three pennies.

As I continued walking through the area where the tables were, there was a nickel on the floor. I then decided to walk through the Food Court. As I was rounding the area, there was a dime on the floor near the elevator. I said thank you Lord for blessing me.

Wednesday, November 9, 2016: At approximately 6:30 am as I was walking through the Customer Information Center (CIC) Food Court during my morning walk, I found a penny near the cashier's register. I said thank you for reminding me of your provisions.

Around 8:15am, I went to the CIC Food Court for Breakfast this morning and ran into Rhonda Tolbert. We talked about the presidential election result and issues related to WFC fraud. I indicated that all our help comes from the Lord. I found a dime on the floor at the counter of the Sbarro Restaurant. I said thank you Jesus.

Sunday, November 13, 2016: I went to the Panthers' game today. We played Kansas City. I left the game at half-time because I had some errands to run. I went to Walmart off Sardis Road, and as I entered the Walmart, I looked into the McDonald's restaurant to the right, and there was a 1987 penny at the entrance to McDonald's. I said thank you Jesus.

Monday, November 14, 2016: Charlie and I went into Starbucks for him to get some coffee. On the way out, I found 1984 penny. I said, "Thank you Jesus".

Tuesday, November 15, 2016: Approximately 8:30am this morning, I went into one of the restrooms and there was a 1963 nickel on the floor. I said, "Thank you Jesus for the reminder that all things come from you."

Sunday, November 20, 2016: After leaving Church today, I went to Walmart on Sardis Road to buy groceries and some miscellaneous items. As I was walking across the parking lot, I found a penny. I said, "Thank you Jesus".

Tuesday, November 22, 2016: I was doing my morning walk through the CIC Food Court. Approximately 6:25 am, I found 1987 penny near the Sbarro Restaurant. At approximately 6:40 am, I was about to enter the Training Center area, and I found a 2013 penny. At 7:16 am, I received an email that my contract was being extended. At approximately 12:15 pm as I am walking into the cafeteria, I found a 2004 penny.

It appears that the two additional pennies I found today was to cover Wednesday and Thursday of this week, because I did find any those days.

Friday, November 25, 2016: This morning around 6:35a m, as I was walking through the cafeteria, I found a penny on top of one of the tables. I said, "Thank you Jesus".

Saturday, November 26, 2106: This morning I rode to Salley, South Carolina with some friends to attend a "Chitlin" festival. This was the first time I had heard of such a thing. We left Charlotte around 7:30 am this morning, and the drive was approximately 2 hours to Salley. We listened to music, visited vendor booths, danced, etc. Around 5:00 pm, we decided to pack up and head toward out car to go back to Charlotte. On the way to the car, there were a group of people dancing to music. So, we stopped to have our last dance. While dancing on the gravel and rocks, I look down and there was a penny. I picked up the penny (1987) after the dance ended and said, "Thank you Jesus for the reminder that you will supply all of my needs".

Sunday, November 27, 2016: After leaving Church service, I went to the Walmart on Sardis Road to buy some apples. As I started down one of the aisles in the parking lot, the gentleman that was collecting the shopping carts was headed toward me with a slew of shopping carts that appeared not to be in his control. I noticed that there was not enough room for the line of carts and my car to get through that aisle. So, I decided to back up my car and went down the next aisle. This gave the gentleman plenty of room to maneuver the carts, and well as protect my car from potentially being hit. After getting out of the car, I headed toward the entrance of Walmart. I was crossing over several aisles, and my spirit told me to turn left by a particular vehicle. As I turned to go by this vehicle, there was a nickel right beside it. I picked it up and said, "Thank you Jesus".

Monday, November 28, 2016: This morning I found a penny (1985) in the Food Court.

Tuesday, November 29, 2016: Around 6:05 am, I found a penny (2005) near the cash register.   At approximately 8:45 am while standing in line at the cashier, I found two separate pennies (1980, 2016).

Wednesday, November 30, 2016: This morning I found a penny (1980) in the Food Court.

Thursday, December 1, 2016: Found a penny (1991) at the entrance of security turn stall around 6:00am. While walking through the exercise facility hallway, found another penny (1965) around 6:50 am. I said I am receiving all the wealth the universe has for me now. Later that day, I went to the Indian Trail Walmart after work. As I was dropping off the shopping cart, I found a penny (2011).

Sunday, December 4, 2016: A Penny (1989) was stuck in between the closet door in my washroom and had probably been there since I had moved in the house in 2003. The house was built in 1989.

Tuesday, December 6, 2016: While walking through Great Wolfe Lodge at a conference I found a penny (1984) while walking through the hallway. After the conference, I went to Walmart to pick-up a few items. I found a dime (2014) in parking lot when returning to my car.

Saturday, December 10, 2016: Today I went to Walmart on Sardis Road to get my brother a pair of Sneakers. After leaving the store, I found a quarter as I was crossing the parking lot.

Monday, December 12, 2016: Found a penny (2005) on the top of a desk in an empty cubicle as I was walking through the aisles at the company I was working at.

Tuesday, December 13, 2016: While walking to the Cafeteria, I passed by and spoke to this gentleman that had just come out of the Wells Fargo bank. He did not notice me. It appeared he was recounting his money. As our paths crossed, a dime (year 2003) rolled across the walkway. I picked it up and looked back to see if he had noticed it falling, and he did not. So, after getting a salad from the Cafeteria, I was headed back to my office and I noticed another dime (year 2016) in the same walkway but was closer to the wall. I picked it up and said, "Thank you Jesus".

Friday, December 16, 2016: After completing my morning walk, someone had dropped a slew of Halls cough drops and candy at the bottom of the stairs in the food court. I picked them up and put them on the table. After walking up the steps to my office and entering through the double doors, I found a penny (1984), as a reminder of God's goodness. I had passed through this same door twice this morning but had not seen the penny earlier.

Sunday, December 18, 2016: I went to QT Gas Station to get gas today, and I needed to use the restroom. After coming out of the restroom, I noticed a penny on the floor below the checkout counter. I picked it up and headed out to my car. I also went to Walmart today, and as I entered the store, there was a penny on the other side of the McDonald's entrance.

Tuesday, December 20, 2016: As I am waiting to get an egg at the Food Court, a penny (1990) was on the floor under the counter where I was standing.

Monday, December 26, 2016: I went to Walmart on Eastern Blvd in Montgomery, Alabama. When I went into the store, I found a penny near the Red Box machine. After coming out of the store, I put the food I had purchased into my car, and then return the shopping carts to one of its locations. I had parked near a Trailblazer truck in the lot, and as I was walking back to my car from returning the shopping cart, I picked up a penny near this truck.

Thursday, January 5, 2017: I went to Walmart today, and as I am leaving the store through the exit doors, there was a quarter and two nickels right outside the entrance of the building.

Saturday, January 14, 2017: I went to Isaiah game at the Mecklenburg Recreational Center. As I am crossing the parking lot headed towards the entrance, I noticed a penny in the parking lot. I picked it up and thanked the Lord for the constant reminder of his provisions.

Later that day, I went to Walmart and on the way out of the store, there was a quarter and a nickel on the outside of the entrance. "Thank you, Jesus,".

Sunday, January 15, 2017: I went to Walmart to buy a lock for the storage unit. I was on the phone talking to my sister as I arrived in the parking lot. I decided to take a seat on the bench and finish our conversation before going into the store. As I was getting up from the bench, I looked back and there were two nickels under the bench where I was sitting. I went into the store to purchase the items I had come for, and as I was going up and down the aisles, I noticed a penny under one of the racks. I picked it up. I then went to the register to check out. As I am walking past other check-out registers that were not open, I noticed two pennies on the floor. I picked them up also. A few feet later, I see this dime in my path. There was this lady heading towards me that spotted the dime also, but she would have had to wait until I passed by it to pick it up because my shopping cart was in that lane. I politely pushed my cart up to the dime and picked it up and kept moving.

Monday, January 16, 2017: I went to Walmart to buy some storage boxes. As I am walking to the restroom in the back of the store, I noticed a nickel (2004). I picked it up and said, "Thank you Jesus".

Wednesday, January 18, 2017: I went to get my BMW washed today. After going through the car wash machine, I pulled into one of the spaces to vacuum my car out. I found a dime beside my car, and then a penny in front of the next parking space to the left of my car.
Later that day, I went to Captain Steve 's Restaurant in Form Mill, SC for dinner. I call a friend to see if he wanted me to bring him a "to-go" dinner. We decided to meet at Lynn's Dance Club on North Tryon Street for him to get the carry-out dinner. As I am waiting for him to meet me at Lynn's, I decided to get some steps in and walk back and forth within the parking lot. There was a dime that was right besides my car in the parking space I had parked in. As I continued to walk within the parking lot, I found a penny, then another penny. I said that "Thank You Lord" for reminding me that all things come from you and I am continually blessed.

Friday, January 20, 2017: I went to AMC movies today to see the "Sleepless" and "Hidden Figures" movies. After I parked my car under the tree, I looked back at my car and noticed a penny in the mud near my front passenger tire. After leaving the movies, I went to DSW to use my $10 coupon. I was talking to my sister on the phone before I went into the store, so I decided to get some steps in outside of the store while I was talking on the phone. As I was walking back and forward along the front of the stores near DSW, I found a penny near the DSW store.

Saturday, January 21, 2017: I went by the Public Storage area to drop off a load at the storage room. I left the storage building and went to QT to get gas for my Volvo. I decided to walk around my car while the gas was pumping, and I found a penny in front of my car.

Monday, January 23, 2017: I decided to go to a different Harris Teeter today. It was on Idlewild Road. As I am walking toward the entrance, I found a 2016 nickel. I later went to Carolina Place Mall to walk and found a penny outside of the Kay Jewelry store. While riding up the escalator in the Dillard's store, I saw a penny on top of one of the Michael Kors' display. Was wondering how a penny got all the way up there. I said, "thank you Lord for all the blessing".

Tuesday, January 24, 2017: I went to Concord Mills Mall today to walk. As soon as I got out of my car, there was a 2016 penny in an empty space beside my car. As I am walking in the mall, I found a 2011 dime outside of the Sea-life Aquarium. Later during the walk, I found another 1960 penny near the movie displays near the AMC movie theater in the mall.

I went to Walmart after getting my car inspected. Found a 1989 penny in the parking lot at the Sardis Road store. I used the self-check out to pay for my groceries. As I am leaving the register, found a 2017 penny.

Friday, January 27, 2017: I went to Carolina Place Mall to walk today. I found a 1994 penny in the Food Court in front of McAlister Deli. As I was rounding the food court, I found a 2008 nickel in front of Sarku Japanese restaurant. Then later while walking the mall, I found 3 shiny pennies (2016) in front of Auntie Annie.

Sunday, January 29, 2017: Isaiah and I went to Concord Mills Mall to walk today. As we were heading toward the entrance to the AMC Movie theatre door, I found a penny. As we are walking by the counter to the AMC movie theatre, I found a dime. I told Isaiah that there is money everywhere, so he needs to start looking for it. So, Isaiah found a penny near Dave and Buster, then one near the ice cream stand, and a third one near Cinnamon Bond restaurant. I found a second penny on my second round in the mall at the AMC movie counter.

Thursday, February 2, 2017: I went to Carolina Place Mall to walk today because the Levine Senior Citizen facility was being closed due to a power outage around 10:00 am. As I am walking the mall, I found a 2015 dime near the Zucsac Restaurant on the lower level. As I am making my last round, I noticed a 2015-Delaware quarter under the counter of the Japanese Sushi Restaurant stand that is outside the food court.

Tuesday, February 7, 2017: As I was getting of my car in the Employment Security Commission parking lot, there was a penny outside of my car.

Wednesday, February 8, 2017: I found a penny at the Indian Trails Walmart today.

Tuesday, February 14, 2017: Found a 2016 penny at the Walmart Forest Bank counter on the floor on my way out of the Walmart.

Wednesday, February 15, 2017: Found a dime in the Walmart parking lot at Indian Trails.

Saturday, February 18, 2017: Nicole had invited me over to her house for a get together. As I am getting out of my car, I found three pennies in the parking lot.

Sunday, February 19, 2017: Before going to church this morning, I found a nickel in Harris Teeter parking lot after coming out of store around 9:15 am.

Wednesday, February 22, 2017: Went to Total Wine today to get some wine for the Yoga, Arts and Wine event that I had planned for March 11th, I found a penny in the parking lot.

Sunday, February 26, 2017: At Carolina Place mall, I found a quarter and a penny in Macy's at one of the sales counters. Then as I was walking through the food court, I found two dimes. Later, I found another dime at the back entrance of the mall. As I am circling the food court, I found a nickel under Panera Bread counter. After getting into my car, and leaving the parking lot, I saw something shiny in one of the parking spaces, I stopped and got out of my car, and there was two dimes and two pennies.

Friday, March 4, 2017: I went to the movie theatre today, and found a penny at the counter.

Tuesday, March 7, 2017: I went to the Park on Monroe Road to walk today. As I am walking around the Lake, I found a penny. After leaving the park, I went to Walmart on Sardis road and found another penny in the parking lot.

Saturday, March 25, 2017: I went to Lewis Financial Real Estate class today to obtain my continuing education credits. Prior to the start of the class, I decided to walk in the development. First, I found a penny, then a nickel and a penny, then another penny, and then a fourth penny as I walked throughout the development.

Sunday, March 26, 2017: I went to a Mexican Restaurant to eat today, and there was a penny under the table where I was seated.

Friday, March 31, 2017: I took Isaiah to see the "Boss Baby" movie at Concord Mills Mall. When I got out of the car, I found two quarters in the parking space where I had parked in the movie theatre parking lot.

Saturday, April 1, 2017: I went to the movie theatre on South Blvd. After the movie, I decided to walk through the parking lot to get some steps in. I found a quarter, then a penny. I then went to Carolina Place mall and I found two pennies near Aunt Annie stand.

Friday, April 7, 2017: I went to Discount Tires to get my tires rotated around 9:30 am this morning. As I walked across the parking lot to the entrance door, I found a dime.

Monday, April 17, 2017: I went to Carolina Place Mall to walk today around 11:00 am. I found a dime in the food court, a penny while on the top level, and a second penny on the top level. I notice a quarter that somehow ended up on the ledge of a window seal on the upper level.

I am convinced that money is waiting to be materialized for our use. If you look for money, you will find it.

Tithing

Malachi 3: 8-11

> *8. Will a man rob God? Yet ye have robbed me. But ye say, Wherein have we robbed thee? In tithes and offerings.*
> *9. Ye are cursed with a curse; for ye have robbed me, even this whole nation.*
> *10. Bring yea all the tithes into the storehouse that there may be meat in mine house, and prove me now herewith, saith the Lord of hosts, if I will not open you the windows of heaven, and pour you out a blessing, that there shall not be room enough to receive it.*
> *11. And I will rebuke the devourer for your sakes, and he shall not destroy the fruits of your ground; neither shall your vine cast her fruit before the time in the field, saith the Lord of hosts.*

Over the last several months during 2016, I had not been paying my tithes consistently and fully. After paying my bills, I felt that I didn't have enough money to cover all my expenses as well as pay my tithes. Every month there was some new expense that surfaced that put me back even further (e.g., new liner for the pool, car repairs, helping with expenses of a family member, etc.). I was taking inventory of my life, wondering what was going on. As I had been listening to audio books and reading books, the topic of tithing would continue come up.

Tithing Convictions

The last few months, I had been "slack" in paying my tithes because I felt like my money was really tight, forgetting that all I have comes from the Lord, and that he will supply my every need. So that Sunday in October 2016, I paid my full 10% on my gross income in tithes. The following Sunday, I did not attend Church, however, I went ahead and wrote the check out, so that the next time I do attend, I will be putting that check in the collection plate.

During the month of October 2016, I decided to write out my tithing check every week after I got paid. Of course, I did not put the check in the collection plate, because I was waiting to see the money in my account. I was over 6 weeks behind in tithing. I didn't attend Church on the last

Sunday in October 2016 because I was out of town. I had told myself that I would bring those checks that I had written for my tithes to church on this Sunday, November 6, 2016. I had 4 checks to put in the collection plate.

As I released the checks from my hand, I asked the Lord to be my immediate and infinite supply. Today, November 6, 2016, we had holy communion where we partook of the bread and wine in remembrance of our Lord and Savior.

Surprisingly, when the Pastor got up to preach today, he indicated that he had never preached a full sermon on this topic before but had preached around it over the last 40 years. The topic was on "Tithing". I felt that this sermon was especially for me, considering what I had been going through for the last several months, and my decision to bring all my tithes into the storehouse today.

After the sermon, the Pastor had an altar call of anyone that wanted to start all over and recommit themselves to tithing. I rushed to the altar, because I feel the Lord was speaking to me directly. I believe he will supply all my needs according to his riches in glory.

Back to Work

My contract job at Wells Fargo ended December 2016. I had been without a job for three months. I received and accepted a job offer in Miami Florida during April 2017, but later withdrew my acceptance. I had felt that moving to Miami was not the direction I needed to be going in.

I was believing that the Lord has opened some awesome doors for me somewhere else so that I can prosper in all that I do and stay on the course of my life goals. During this time, I also found out that my daughter was pregnant with her second child. I was trying to figure out the driving distance from Miami to Raleigh, NC. How often would I visit or how often would they visit me in Miami.

In April 2017, I attended some friends' anniversary and retirement party. Two other friends mentioned that they were going to another party after leaving this anniversary and retirement party. I asked them if it would be ok if I went with them to this party, and they said it was ok. I later found out the owner of the home was an Audit Director at a multi-media company. I sent her my resume while at her home. Approximately, one month later, I received a call from a placement company looking to fill a contract position at this same multi-media company under this Audit Director. I got the position and started to work July 2017.

Motivation: _How to Reach Your Full Potential? God's Plan for My Life (A Balance Schedule)_

1. _Begin your day with the Lord_
2. _Spend time with family and friends_
3. _You need Gods perspective about your work_
4. _Spend time in worship at Church_

5. *You need rest and relaxation*
6. *Spend time on fitness and health*
7. *You need fun and recreation*
8. *Contemplate surrounding yourself with the condition you want to produce*
9. *Plan to live your life on purpose*
10. *In my world, nothing ever goes wrong*

To reach your full potential, you must have a clean heart, clear mind, balance schedule, rest, health and fitness. Things that Hinder Your Potential:

1. *Divided mind*
2. *Slothfulness*
3. *The influence of other people*
4. *Neglecting private time with God*
5. *Lack of Commitment*
6. *Lack of Discipline*
7. *A wrong sense of values*
8. *Misplaced Priorities*
9. *Unbridled ambition – inner need to work yourself to death to reach world standards*

By Dr. Wayne Dyer

Income During Decade 6

Year	Source	Amount
2010	TITACS	36,495.02
2011	TITACS, Carolina Healthcare System	82,268.20
2012	TITACS, Carolina Healthcare System	96,752.13
2013	TITACS, Carolina Healthcare System	78,168.15
2014	TITACS, Contracts	98,680.67
2015	TITACS, Contracts	127,267.37
2016	Contracts	106,385.88
2017	Passive Income	18,113.30
2018	Heavens' Highway, Inc.	49,599.26
2019	Heaven's Highway, Inc., Contracts	110,000.00
	Total	**$ 803,729.98**

Motivation: *The Lord's ways are not our ways, and there are infinite resources.*

I just turned 60 as I close this book. I wanted to take this opportunity to thank you for reading part of my life's journey. I trust that the book has been a motivator and an inspiration to you. My story does not end here as I turn the pages into the next decade of my life. Remember, the power is with you!!

60 Goals
(Things I want to Accomplish)

After reading Jack Canfield's books on the Success Principles, he mentioned the story of a man that had written 101 things he wanted to do before he dies. Jack also indicated he had a list of 101 and recommended everyone take the time to do this. So, I started my list 9/18/2016 and here is my list of 60:

1. I want a silver Diablo Lamborghini.
2. I want to make an additional $100,000 in income and $100,000 every week thereafter.
3. I want to be blissfully and happily married.
4. I want to own a Lear Jet and have access to a helicopter.
5. I want to become a billionaire, with a net worth of $5 billion at least.
6. I want to sale my current home immediately.
7. I want to develop products that will serve humanity.
8. I want to pay off all my immediate family's debt.
9. I want to be an inspiration for single Mothers.
10. I want to lose down to 140 pounds.
11. I want my next home to have 5 bedrooms, 4-car garage with a building with 3 additional bays for vehicles, 2 offices, conference room, double staircase in the front entrance of house, and a separate staircase from the back, lap pool, sauna, hot tub, library, media room, view of the water from the balcony on the back of the house, marble flooring in the entrance, two entrances into property with automated gates, property enclosed in a brick wall approximately 5-6 feet high.
12. I want to be interviewed by Oprah Winfrey on my new bestselling book.
13. I want to visit the Taj Mahal in India.
14. I want to be a Motivational Speaker and speak to thousands about the "Power of the Mind".
15. I want perfect health.
16. I want to attend Anthony Robinson conference in 2017 *(Completed)*.

I had planned to go to one of Tony's Peak Performance conferences in San Diego, CA during October 2017. I had checked hotel and plane reservation, etc. Since I started back to work, my schedule suddenly became full. I then decided that maybe I will try to attend the session he had in Florida in December 2017. I was thinking that my contract job would be ended the early part of December and I can easily arrange this.

Nevertheless, while traveling on I-485 one Sunday with my daughter and grandson, I noticed a billboard that said Marcus Sarmonis and Tony Robbins live in Charlotte, NC. I immediately went on the internet to get the detail. They were going to be in Charlotte, NC the next Thursday, October 19, 2017 at the Bojangles arena. I immediately registered to attend.

While at the NAC – National Achievers Congress, Tony mentioned that it had been over 10 years since he had been in Charlotte. They had planned this NAC for Houston, Texas but due to Hurricane Harvey the congress was canceled. So, Tony indicated that they were trying to decide where to host it, and since he had not been to Charlotte in a while, they decided to have it in Charlotte.

So, the moral of the story is that instead of me trying to figure out how to see Tony Robbins, the Lord and Universe brought him to me, whereas the location was approximately 6 miles from my home. "The Power that is Within You".

17. I want to travel to every continent at least once (e.g., *Africa, Europe*, Asia, South America, Antarctica, Australia, *North America*).
18. I want to write a Bestseller book and sale a minimum of 5 million copies, within 6 months after publishing.
19. I would like to have a conversation with President Barack Obama about his challenges while President.
20. I want to take a vacation in Dubai, with my husband.
21. I want to visit TD Jakes church or attend one of his conferences.
22. I want a vacation home in Monaco, Monte Carlo and a yacht.
23. I want to have dinner with Warren Buffett.
24. I want to learn to speak French.
25. I want to visit the Great Wall of China.
26. I want my 'Bestseller" book to be entitled: **From Welfare to a Millionaire (***The Greatness That Lies Within You***)**
27. I want to join the Millionaire Club.
28. I want to visit the Eiffel Tower in Paris France *(Completed)*.
29. I want me and my husband to take difference dance lessons together.
30. I want to help change the thinking of millions of people so that they can realize that the Lord has put everything we need within us.
31. I want to develop, design and distribute product around the world.
32. I want to learn to speak Spanish.
33. I want to be one of the "400 Wealthiest Persons in America".
34. I want to learn to swim confidently.
35. I want to read a book every 2 week.
36. I want a license/contract agreement with five of the top 11 car manufacturers for my products. They are listed below:

     a. Toyota – Japanese (Toyota, Aichi)
     b. Ford – Dearborn, Michigan
     c. Honda – Japanese
     d. General Motors – Detroit Michigan
     e. Volkswagon – German
     f. PSA Peugeot Citroen – French
     g. Nissan – Japanese
     h. Hyundai – South Korea
     i. Renault – French (Boulogne – Billancourt)
     j. Suzuki – Japanese
     k. BMW -German

37. I want season tickets to the Carolina Panthers games (*Completed: November 2016*).
38. I want to see Serena Williams play a match of tennis (US Open or French Open).
39. I want to finish my idea I had regarding the shoe.
40. I want to patent idea "Leaf".
41. I want to learn to speak German.
42. I want to attend the Kentucky Derby. *(Completed: May 1-5, 2019)*
43. I want to sell over $100 million in real estate in two years.
44. I want to design the website for Heaven's Highway, Inc.
45. I want to write my second-best seller book, "Letters – The Challenges".
46. I want to become B-I-C (Broker-In-Charge) eligible.
47. I want to start up my own real estate company, TRIXS (Thornton Real-estate Investment Xceptional Services, Inc.).
48. I want Tyler Perry to produce a movie of my life, "From Welfare to Millionaire"
49. I want to learn how to play piano/organ by completing lessons and/or using an app.
50. I want to patent idea "SAM".
51. I want to patent idea "Capsule Mobile".
52. I want to patent idea "Spoken Words".
53. I want to learn to speak Arabic.
54. I want to view the Indian Ocean from my balcony.
55. I want to view the Arctic Ocean from my balcony.
56. I want to view the Atlantic Ocean from my balcony.
57. I want to view the Pacific Ocean from my balcony.
58. I want to be a good steward of all my blessings.
59. I want to view Niagara Falls.
60. I want to have life and have it more abundantly.

Motivation: When you want something, all the universe rises to meet you to achieve it, but you must have clarity.

1. The Holy Bible
2. The Miracle of Mind Dynamics by Joseph Murphy, D.D., D.R.S., Ph.D., LL. D
3. Psycho-Cybernetics 2000 by Maxwell Maltz, Bobbe Sommer
4. Manifest Your Destiny (The Nine Spiritual Principles for Getting Everything you Want) by Wayne W. Dyer
5. Real Magic (Creating Miracles in Everyday Life) by Dr. Wayne W. Dyer
6. Thoughts are Things by Prentice Mulford
7. Reposition Yourself (Living Life Without Limits) by T.D. Jakes
8. Ask and It Is Given (The Teaching of Abraham) by Esther and Jerry Hicks
9. Empowering Yourself (The Organizational Game Revealed) by Harvey J Coleman
10. Spontaneous Healing by Andrew Weil, M.D.
11. The Great Investment (Faith, Family and Finance) by T.D. Jakes
12. The Purpose Driven Live (What on Earth Am I Here For?) by Rick Warren
13. Unlimited Power by Anthony Robbins
14. The Magic of Getting What You Want by David J. Schwartz
15. Fresh Vegetable and Fruit Juices (What's Missing in Your Body?) by Dr. N, W Walker
16. Unexpected Miracles (The Gift of Synchronicity and How to Open It) by David Richo, Ph.D.
17. JESUS CEO (Using Ancient Wisdom for Visionary Leadership) by Laurie Beth Jones
18. The Fourth Dimension (Discovering a New World of Answered Prayer) by Dr. David Yonggi Cho
19. Dancing in the Arms of God (Finding Intimacy and Fulfillment by Following His Lead) by Connie Neal
20. Anointing Fall on Me (Accessing the Power of the Holy Spirit) by T. D. Jakes
21. A Divine Revelation of Heaven by Mary k. Baxter
22. 8 Weeks to Optimum Health by Andrew Weil, M.D.
23. The Power of Self-Esteem by Nathaniel Branden, Ph.D.
24. Battlefield of the Mind by Joyce Myers
25. The Miracle of Fasting by Bragg
26. The Millionaire Next Door by Thomas J. Stanley, PhD., William D. Danko, PhD.
27. All Thoughts are Creative – The Power of the Mind by John Kehoe
28. Single, Married, Separated, and Life After Divorce by Miles Munroe
29. Living in Divine Health (It's Never too Late to Form Healthier Habits) by Don Colbert, MD
30. The Celestine Prophecy (An Adventure) by James Redfield
31. Change Your Thoughts – Change Your Life by Dr. Wayne W. Dyer
32. Do You! (12 Laws to Access the Power in You to Achieve Happiness and Success) by Russell Simmons with Chris Morrow
33. Health Wise Handbook (A Self-Care Manual For You) by Donald W. Kemper

34. Patent It Yourself by Patent Attorneys David Pressman & Thomas J. Tuytschaevers
35. The Power of I AM by Joel Osteen
36. The Independent Inventor's Handbook by Louis J. Foreman and Jill Gillbert Welytok
37. Talk Your Way to an Intimate Marriage by Donald Harvey
38. Getting the Love You Want (A Guide for Couples) by Harville Hendrix, Ph.D.
39. The Magic of Believing (The Science of Setting Your Goal and Then Reaching It) by Claude M. Bristol
40. Custom-Fix Husband Ready-Made Wife (A Woman's Guide to Molding Her Mate) by LaQuenta Clarke.
41. Inventing for Dummies by Pamela Riddle Bird, PhD.
42. Think Like a Man Act Like A Lady by Steve Hardy
43. How to Manifest Your Desires by Neville Goddard
44. Be What You Wish by Neville Goddard
45. Feeling is the Secret by Neville Goddard
46. Metaphysics Anthology by Neville Goddard
47. The Secret by Rhonda Byrne
48. The Success Principles (How to Get from Where you are to Where You Want to Be) by Jack Canfield
49. Think and Grow Rich by Napoleon Hill
50. Think and Grow Rich: A Black Choice by Dennis Kimbro
51. The Silva Mind Control of Mental Dynamics (You can Unleash the Power of Your Mind to Solve Any Problem) by Jose' Silva and Burt Goldman
52. The Power of your Subconscious Mind, by Dr. Joseph Murphy
53. The Power of Spoken Blessings by Bill Gothard
54. Small Miracles II (Heartwarming Gifts of Extraordinary Coincidences) by Yitta Halberstam & Judith Leventhal
55. Small Miracles for Women (Extraordinary Coincidences of Heart and Spirit) by Yitta Halberstam & Judith Leventhal
56. How to Open the Door to your Future by Dan Kennedy
57. A Life God Rewards by Bruce Wilkinson with David Kopp
58. My Utmost for His Highest (Classic Daily Devotional) by Oswald Chambers
59. The Dancing Wu Li Masters (An Overview of the New Physics) by Gary Zukav
60. You are the Universe by Deepak Chopra and Menas C. Kafatos

This book is an inspiration to anyone that feels life has thrown them some low blows. We have all been granted gifts and ideas. Our challenge is to move forward and take that first step, and the universe will meet you to achieve it. You must decide what it is you want, and just start doing it.

Abbie Thornton is a CPA, CISA, PMP with over 30 years of experience specializing in providing consulting services in the Information Technology arena. An Alabama State University graduate that has started up two companies. She currently lives in Charlotte, North Carolina.

THE END

Made in the USA
Middletown, DE
09 January 2020